Sprednje lice

Nadstropje

Hodnik

SLOVENIAN
COOKING

140 RECIPES

Stransko lice

Pritličje

SLOVENIAN COOKING
Tekst: Andrej A. Fritz
Fotos and Design: Matjaž Chvatal
Ilustration: Albert Sić
Translated by: Simona Pečnik-Kržič

Založba Turistika, 2001
Za založbo: Mira Chvatal

Založba Turistika
Trstenik 101
4204 Golnik
++386 (0)4 25-60-110
E-mail: zalozba@turistika.net
http://www.zalozba-turistika.si

CIP - Kataložni zapis o publikaciji
Narodna in univerzitetna knjižnica, Ljubljana

641.5(497.4)(083.1)

FRITZ, Andrej A.
    Slovenian Cooking : 140 Recipes / (tekst: Andrej A. Fritz ;
fotos Matjaž Chvatal ; ilustration Albert Sić ; translated by Simona Pečnik-
Kržič). - Kranj : Turistika, 2001

ISBN 961-6414-00-3
1. Gl. stv. nasl.
112946944

Morning mists are still swirling through the valleys while mountain peaks adorned with the rays of the morning sun are bathing in the first light of dawn. Spring is in the air. The last patches of snow in the ravines are slowly disappearing, and in shady corners, primroses are already in full blossom while meadow saffron and snowdrops shyly begin to peek from the ground. Grey smoke is pouring from the chimney of an old farm house where a bundle of wood is crackling in the old farm stove.

In the bowl on a stone shelf by the stove is half risen yeast mixture ready to be kneaded into dough for bread and potica. In the black hall at the other side of the fireplace, ham, sausages and bacon, all prepared by the butcher the previous week, are hanging from the ceiling. They are already slightly cured and their attractive smell permeates the air.

I put two more beech logs into the old stove and the water begins to boil. Mother puts in two pinches of salt and waits until it is boiling vigorously, then pours in a cup of buckwheat flour and makes a hole in the centre with a wooden spoon handle. Hot water erupts like a volcano. She pulls the pot to the side of the stove and leaves it to simmer gently. In the meantime, the sweet smell of coffee fills the room. She takes melted cracklings and sprinkles them on crumbled buckwheat žganci. Chicken soup is boiling in a big pot and home-made noodles are drying on a wooden tray near the stove. Mother is still busy in the kitchen preparing the gibanica, and before lunch delicious smelling zelan bread and potica are taken out of the stove. Hungry mouths are already looking forward to budlan tongue, mežerli and štruklji.

Every mention of traditional cooking stirs up a memory of that melange of smells. The different regions of Slovenia; Primorska, Notranjska, Dolenjska, Štajerska, Prekmurje, The Ljubljana Region and Gorenjska offer a great variety of dishes. Every season brings different delicacies. Religious holidays, national customs, birthdays, different feasts and influences from neighbouring countries also leave their mark in the country's rich and varied culinary chest.

In this tiny book you'll find only a small selection of Slovenian dishes. Housewives have made their own varieties of similar recipes. Maybe you won't follow the recipes word by word but include or omit some ingredients to suit your own taste. That is fine; in essence, the dish will still be the same. Tastes differ.

I wish you a bundle of culinary joys with 'Slovenian Cooking' and hope that you enjoy the results!

Your chef,
Andrej A. Fritz

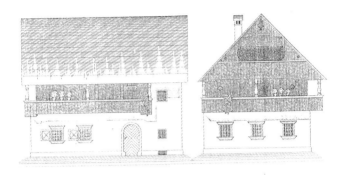

SOUPS

Every nation has different ways of preparing food. This is true of soups as well. Soups in Slovenia are varied in taste, depending on their region of origin where different vegetables grow and soups are enriched with local herbs and spices.

Brown Soup
Soup vegetables (carrots, parsley root, 1/2 onion, bay leaf, 1 garlic clove, 1 turnip slice, celery, 1 kale leaf), few pepper corns, 1 tablespoon lard, 1/2 kg beef, 100 g liver, 200 g veal parings, 2 litres beef soup.

Melt the lard in a saucepan, add the sliced carrots, parsley, yellow turnip, celery, onion, kale, liver, lean beef, bones and veal parings, and fry until coloured. Add the beef soup, bring to the boil and cook gently for 1 hour. If you want a very clear soup, pass it through a clean piece of cloth. Serve with trimmings or on its own in a soup bowl.

Broth
3/4 kg meat, 1/4 kg bones, carrots, celery, parsley, onion, 200 g beef liver, 40g butter or lard, salt, pepper corns, bay leaf, saffron.

Rinse 3/4 kg of good quality beef and some bones with medulla. Put it all in a pot and add 2 litres of cold water. Bring to the boil and leave the brown foam which appears on the top of the soup to make it stronger. The foam will eventually sink. Then add the salt, onion, carrots, parsley, celery and cabbage stem. Alternatively, you can chop the vegetables with some liver and mix it all together with some butter or lard until golden brown, then add to the broth to give it a nice yellow colour. Cook the meat gently for about 2 hours. When the meat is cooked, pour a teacup of cold water into the soup to make it clearer, and leave it for a while to cool. Pass it through a fine strainer.

Beef soup is made from a piece of beef, beef bones, soup vegetables and herbs. It has to simmer gently and be covered so that its aroma does not evaporate. If it boils too fiercely, it becomes turbid and the meat is hard and stringy. If the emphasis is on the soup, the meat should be put in cold water and brought to the boil slowly. However, if the emphasis is on the taste of the meat, put it in boiling water.

Chicken Soup with Meatballs

1 chicken (around 1kg), soup vegetables (carrots, parsley root, 1/2 onion, bay leaf, 1 garlic clove, 1 turnip slice, celery, 1 kale leaf), bay leaf, 2 cl cognac

For the dumplings: 300 g cooked chicken meat, 2 eggs, 50 g white bread soaked in 100 ml warm milk, 1 tablespoon chopped fresh chives

For the soup: Put the chicken and soup vegetables into a pot, add water and simmer until tender. Bone the chicken. Mince the meat in a food processor, then add the soaked bread, fried onion, chopped chives, eggs and Cognac. Mix well and form the mixture into walnut sized balls. Cook them in 1/3 of the soup. Put the soup into bowls, season to taste and add the meatballs.

National soups – regional characteristics
Every nation has different ways of preparing food. This is also true of soups. In Slovenia, soups are usually served as starters. They are characterised by the numerous varieties and their pleasant taste.

Bela Krajina Potato Soup

1/2 kg potatoes, 100 ml soup, 200 ml cream, 2 tablespoons flour, vinegar, salt, pepper, sugar, marjoram;

Peel, dice, wash and cook the potatoes in salted water. Mix the flour to a paste with the cream and gradually blend in 100 ml of soup to avoid lumps, then pour slowly into the soup, stirring constantly. Season to taste with sugar, vinegar, salt and marjoram and simmer for a few more minutes.

Ljubljana Escargots Soup

4 dozen escargots, 60 g butter, 2 shallots, 1.5 litre beef soup, nutmeg, 3 egg yolks, 50 ml dry white wine;

Clean the escargots first by cooking them gently in salted water for 1 hour. Remove them from their shells with a fork and discard the black skin. Sprinkle them with salt to melt away any slime, then drain and rinse them thoroughly. Squeeze out all the water. It is also possible to use canned escargots, available in shops. You need about 4 dozen washed escargots. Finely chop half of them. Melt the butter in a pan, add finely chopped shallots and fry until soft but not coloured. Add the chopped escargots and cook gently for a while. Pour in the beef soup, season with freshly ground nutmeg and bring to the boil. Add the remaining escargots. Finally, beat the eggs with some cold soup, pour into the soup and add some toasted bread slices.

Carniolan Crayfish in Soup

1 litre beef soup, 1 dozen crayfish, 100 g butter, 30 g flour;

First, make good beef broth. To feed four, take a dozen large crayfish and boil them for 15 minutes. Take the flesh from the claws and tail, then crush the shells. Melt 100g of butter in a saucepan, add the crushed shells and fry until the butter turns reddish. Add a tablespoon of flour and pour in 1 litre of soup. Then pass through a very fine strainer. Before serving, bring the soup to the boil again, simmer for 5 minutes and add the crayfish tails. The soup should not be too thick. The same is true for any soup, served at social occasions.

Prežganka with Eggs

100 ml oil, 80 g flour, 4 eggs, salt, caraway seed, water;

Heat the oil in a saucepan, add flour, briefly fry, pour in the water and bring to the boil. Season with caraway seed and salt. Simmer for 10 minutes, beat the eggs and slowly pour them into the soup. Serve hot.

Potučnca - Fish Soup

4 trout, 1 onion, 4 garlic cloves, 2 parsley sprigs, lovage sprig, marjoram, carrots, pepper corns, 50 g butter, salt.

Bring salted water to the boil and add the herbs, vegetables and the gutted trout. Simmer for 10 minutes until the trout are cooked, then take them from the pot and cool. Discard the skin and bones. Filter the soup and finely chop the cooked vegetables and herbs. Melt the butter in a saucepan, gently fry the onions, then add the vegetables and pour into the soup. Bring to the boil and add a fistful of ribana kaša. After a few minutes, add the trout and sprinkle with fresh chopped parsley.

Sour Pork Soup

1 kg pork feet and tail, 500 g soup vegetables, 250 g potatoes, salt, 5 garlic cloves, pepper, bay leaf, marjoram, vinegar.

Wash the feet and tail and chop into smaller pieces. Cook in about 2.5 litres of salted water for about 45 minutes. Remove the foam and add the bay leaf and marjoram. Then, add the chopped vegetables (carrots, celery, turnip, cabbage) and potatoes. Add a beef stock cube to improve the taste. When the meat and vegetables are cooked, fry 2 tablespoons of flour in some oil, then add chopped garlic and pour into the soup. Simmer for a while. Remove the pot from the stove, add a tablespoon of sour cream, a tablespoon of vinegar and stir. Pour into a tureen and sprinkle with chopped parsley or chives.

Koroška Wedding Soup

1 kg pork feet, soup vegetables (carrots, parsley root, 1/2 onion, bay leaf, 1 garlic clove, 1 turnip slice, celery, 1 kale leaf), 1/2 litre sour cream, 50 g flour, 1-2 egg yolks.

Cook the pork feet with vegetables in salted water until tender. Remove the feet and blend into a mixture, made of flour and half of the sour cream. Bring to the boil, then blend in the remaining sour cream, mixed with egg yolks. Before serving, remove the meat from the bones, chop it and add to the soup.

Cream Soup with Buckwheat and Boletus

250 g husked buckwheat, 250 g frozen or 50 g dried boletus, 30 g lard, 1 onion, 100 ml cream, 1 tablespoon flour, 3 garlic cloves, parsley, thyme, marjoram, salt pepper.

Wash the buchwheat and cook it in 1 litre of water for 30 minutes. Just before the water boils add the sliced mushrooms. If you use dried mushrooms, first you have to soak them in hot water for a while, and then squeeze out the water of them. Fry the onions and garlic in lard and add to the buckwheat. Put in the herbs and season to taste with salt and pepper. Mix the cream with a tablespoon of flour and blend into the soup when the bucwheat is cooked. Simmer for 15 more minutes, sprinkle with chopped parsley and serve.

Čisava Župa

200 g lamb, 500 g beef, 500 g chicken, 3/4 litre cream, 1 tablespoon of flour, diced white bread, spices: cinnamon crust, ground cinnamon, aniseed, ginger, nutmeg, carrots, saffron, lemon peel, onion, leek, basil, celery, parsley (leaves and root).

Cook all the meat, spices, herbs (except for the ground cinnamon) and vegetables in a 2 litre pot. After about 1 1/2 hours, when the meat is tender, remove it. Mix 3/4 litre of cream with the flour and gradually blend the mixture into the boiling soup, stirring constantly to avoid lumps. Simmer it for 5 more minutes. Chop the meat into small pieces and put into the soup together with diced bread fried in butter. Serve with ground cinnamon.

Chestnut Soup

1 litre bone soup, 250 g cooked chestnuts, 200 ml wine, salt, black pepper, marjoram, basil, vinegar;

Boil the bone soup and add the crushed chestnuts, marjoram, basil, salt, black pepper, wine and vinegar. Leave it to simmer for 15 minutes. This soup was traditionally appreciated by those with a hangover, caused by drinking too much young wine. People still say that chestnut soup clears wine from the head.

STEWS AND HOT POTS
**are usually served on their own for lunch or for
dinner during the week.**

Chicken Stew
1 chicken, soup vegetables, 1 onion, 2 carrots, 1 tomato, 2 tablespoons flour, 3 garlic cloves, 1 glass white wine, thyme, bay leaf, pepper corns, salt.

Make a puppet shape from the vegetables: carrots, celery, leek, parsley, marjoram, thyme, calamint and bay leaf. Use a piece of string or a leek stem. Cook the chicken (roughly chopped) with the puppet, garlic cloves and tomato halves, seasoned with pepper corns and salt. Finely chop the onion and fry until golden brown. Add to the stew. When the chicken is tender, mix 2 tablespoons of flour to a paste with 200 ml of water and gently pour into the stew. Simmer for a few minutes and season with a glass of white wine. You can also add dough balls or žličniki.

Sirnica
250 g bread, 1 litre vegetable soup, salt, parsley, chives, 100 ml cream, 200 g grated cheese;

Cut the bread into pieces and cook it in 500 ml vegetable soup for 10 minutes. Press through a sieve, add the rest of the soup and salt. Cook for another 5 minutes, then stir in the cheese, cream, chives, parsley; bring to the boil and serve hot.

Chamois Stew
2,5 kg chamois meat, 1 kg potatoes, 1 garlic clove, 1 large onion, lard, marjoram, dry arnica, bay leaf, sour cream, egg yolk, white wine, salt, black pepper, carrots, 1 lemon;

Chop the onion and fry it in lard until it changes colour, then add the chopped meat and carrots. Smother for about 30 minutes. Pour in some beef soup and add the sliced potatoes and seasoning. Let it simmer for another hour. When almost done, stir in the sour cream mixed with egg yolk, and the wine. Season to taste.

The Ribnica Alleluia
2 litres smoked meat stock, 300 g husked millet, 300 g fresh or 150 g dried turnip peelings;

Carefully wash the millet. Wash and cook the turnip peelings for about 1 hour, then strain and chop them. Half cook the millet in the meat stock and add the chopped peelings. Simmer until the millet is cooked, then serve on its own with bean salad.

Fowl soup is known for its strengthening qualities and it is usually served at different festive occasions like weddings, or at times of illness.

Štajerska Bean Stew

300 g smoked and 200 g fresh bacon, 500 g beans, 400 g chopped onion, 100 g lard, 20 g crushed garlic, 20 g paprika, 50 g tomato puree, bay leaf, carrot, salt;
Cook the beans. Dice the bacon and fry it in lard together with the chopped onion, smoked bacon and garlic. Add the paprika, bay leaf and grated carrot. Simmer for about half an hour until the bacon is tender, then mix into the beans. Season to taste, bring to the boil, simmer for another 15 minutes and stir in the tomato puree.

Bograč

200 g smoked bacon, 750 g fresh pork, 750 g beef, 1 kg potatoes, 2 kg onion, 2 fresh red peppers, salt, spices;
Finely chop the onion and the bacon then fry them, adding fresh red peppers, cut into pieces, diced meat and water (as necessary) and smother. After an hour add peeled potatoes cut in four, season to taste and cook for another half hour.

Bujta Repa

2 kg sour turnip, 250 g husked millet, 1.5 kg pork back, 100 g lard, 50 g flour, 5 garlic cloves, 1 onion, salt;
Cook the meat and the turnip until almost done, then add the washed husked millet and roux with crushed garlic and chopped onion. Before you stir in the roux, mix it with some water to make it smoother. Simmer the turnip for another 5 minutes. Salt to taste. To serve, cut the meat and arrange the pieces on top of the turnip.
To prepare this dish, you can use fresh or smoked pork.

Ričet

1 kg cured pork neck, 200 g pot barley, 250 g cooked brown beans, soup vegetables (carrots, parsley root, half onion, bay leaf, garlic clove, large slice of turnip, celery, kale leaf), bay leaf;
Cook the meat in a large pan, then take it out of the soup and put in the chopped soup vegetables, bay leaf, pepper corns, few garlic cloves and pot barley. When the pot barley is cooked, stir in the cooked beans and let it simmer for a few more minutes. Season to taste. Ričet should not be too thick. Serve with slices of cured meat.

Skuha

5 large potatoes, 500 g beans, 1 kg sauerkraut, 100 ml oil, 2 tablespoons flour, salt, cracklings;

Soak the beans in water overnight and cook them. Peel and dice the potatoes and cook them with sauerkraut. Make roux with oil and flour and stir it into the cooked sauerkraut. Mix well. Cook for another 5 minutes then put in cooked beans. Cook until the potatoes are done. The dish should not be too watery. Season to taste, bring to the boil and sprinkle with cracklings.

Krhljanka Turnip

500 g turnip, 2 tablespoons flour, salt, cumin, water, 80 g lard, 1 onion, 2 tablespoons cracklings;

Peel, dice and cook the turnip in salted water for about 1 hour. When nearly finished, sprinkle with a pinch of ground cumin and stir in a mixture of flour and water. Cook for a few more minutes. Finely chop the onion and fry it in cracklings. Add to the turnip. Serve with potatoes, žganci or plum dumplings.

Turnip Shoots in Salad

500 g turnip shoots, 500 g potatoes, 1 tablespoon cracklings, garlic, oil, vinegar, salt, black pepper;

Peel, cook and slice the potatoes. Cut the turnip shoots into strips, put them in a bowl and add the hot sliced potatoes, melted cracklings, finely chopped garlic clove, salt and black pepper. Mix the salad and add vinegar.

Baked Broad Beans with Zaseka

1 kg beans – broad beans, 500 g finely chopped onion, 200 g zaseka or cracklings, 2 tomatoes, 1 celery stalk, 1 small bunch parsley, marjoram, thyme, 3 garlic cloves, salt, 1 teaspoon ground paprika, 100 g smoked bacon, 100 ml oil;

Cook the broad beans until tender and strain them. Fry the onion in the zaseka or cracklings until soft but not coloured, then add the diced bacon and tomatoes. Add the cooked broad beans, herbs, chopped garlic, paprika, oil and black pepper to taste. Mix well. Put the mixture in a moderately hot oven until a nice crust is formed. Just before serving, sprinkle evenly with a few tablespoons of sour milk. This dish goes well with apple cider and rye bread.

Country-Style Sauerkraut

1 kg sauerkraut, 1 medium sized onion, 2 garlic cloves, cumin, bay leaf, 4 tablespoons cracklings or zaseka;

Cook the sauerkraut with herbs for 1 hour until half of the water has evaporated and strain it. Chop the onion, fry it in the cracklings until it colours slightly, then add the crushed garlic. Add the onion and garlic to the sauerkraut and boil for another 15 minutes.

Žvarcet

1,5 kg veal, 100 g butter, 50 g bread crumbs, beef soup, nutmeg, thyme, lemon peel, marjoram, parmesan;

Cut the veal into small pieces and smother in butter until tender, adding beef soup occasionally. Fry the bread crumbs in butter and stir them in together with grated lemon peel. Pour in some more soup and let it simmer for a few minutes.

Žvarcet has to be thick. Sprinkle with parmesan and serve hot.

Fried Mushrooms

500 g mushrooms, 50 g lard or olive oil, 1 onion, 4 garlic cloves, 50 g smoked ham, 1 parsley sprig, 30 g grated cheese, soup, black pepper, salt;

Clean, slice and blanch the mushrooms. Finely chop the onion and fry it in lard or olive oil with chopped smoked ham. Stir in the crushed garlic and parsley, fry for a few more minutes and add the mushrooms. Season to taste. Gently simmer for another 10 minutes, occasionally adding some soup. When finished, stir in the grated cheese. To prepare this dish, use boletus, golden or honey agarics or chanterelles.

Kolacija

150 g prunes, 150 g dried pears, 150 g dried apples, 150 g raisins, 150 g dried figs, grated lemon peel, sugar, about 3 litres water, 200 g beans, salt;

Cook the beans in the salted water. In another pot, cook the dried pears for 10 minutes, then add the dried apples, figs and lemon peel and, after 5 minutes, the raisins and prunes. Strain the fruit and the beans and mix in a bowl. Before serving, sprinkle with sugar if you wish.

Beans with Cottage Cheese

250 g cottage cheese, 1 kg cooked salted beans, 100 ml sour cream, salt, chives, chopped parsley;

Mix the cottage cheese, the cream, parsley and chives, then add warm cooked beans. Serve cold.

Cucumbers with Cream

200 ml cream, 2 kg cucumbers, 2 tablespoons flour, about 300 ml water, parsley, black pepper, salt;

Peel the cucumbers and remove the seed, then grate and fry them together with parsley in oil until the water evaporates. Stir in the flour and then about 300 ml water. Simmer for 5 minutes. Mix in the cream and season with salt and black pepper.

Čepenca

250 ml sour cream, 250 ml cream, 8 to 10 tablespoons buckwheat or wheat flour, salt.

Mix together both creams, season with salt and bring to the boil. When it is boiling, mix in the flour and cook, stirring constantly with a wooden spoon, until the čepenca spins together with the spoon. Serve with sour milk or white coffee.

Sauerkraut is a typical Slovene dish served mostly in winter time. It goes best with cured meat and various roasts.

Primorsko Višče

A large bunch of young turnip leaves, 4 garlic cloves, parsley, butter;

Remove the stems, wash the leaves and smother them in some water. When done, strain and chop them. Keep the water in which you cooked the leaves. Heat some butter in a frying pan and add crushed garlic and chopped turnip leaves. Add some water and sprinkle with parsley. Simmer for a few more minutes and serve as a side dish.

Cauliflower Bundle

Dough: 200 g flour, 500 ml water, 1 egg, 1 tablespoon oil;

Stuffing: 1 large cauliflower, 50 g butter, 100 g grated cheese, 100 g cured ham, salt;

Knead a firm dough from the ingredients and leave it to rest for about 1 hour. Half cook the cauliflower. Roll out the dough and put the cauliflower on it. Put small pieces of butter and cured ham between the blossoms, sprinkle with cheese and season with pepper. Wrap the dough as if you were closing a bundle, tying it with a strip of dough. Beat an egg and spread it on the bundle. Bake in the oven at 190°C for 40 minutes.

Sour turnip is just as popular as sauerkraut and is typically found in regional stews. It can be served on its own or as a side dish.

Debelnica

3 medium sized turnips, 6 large potatoes, 150 g zaseka, 5 garlic cloves, salt, pepper;

Wash the turnips and peel the potatoes, then dice and cook them. Strain and mash them and sprinkle with zaseka. Mix well. Serve on its own with sausages or cured meat, or alternatively as a side dish with sauerkraut or smothered cabbage and vegetables.

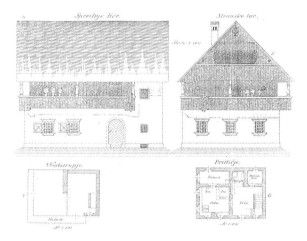

MASOVNIK or MASOVNEK

is a typical shepherd's dish, which can be made in a variety of ways.

Masovnik

200 ml milk, 200 ml sour cream, 3 tablespoons wheat flour, 1 tablespoon corn flour, 1 tablespoon butter, salt;

Fry the flour in butter. In another pot, boil the milk together with sour cream and some salt. Cook until it leaves the sides of the pan, usually about 5 to 10 minutes, stirring vigorously. Serve hot with sour milk.

Masovnek with Sour Milk

500 ml cream, 500 ml sour cream, salt, around 150 g buckwheat or corn flour, 1 egg (optional);

Pour the creams together into a saucepan, season with salt and simmer gently for 10 minutes, stirring constantly to prevent it sticking to the bottom. After 10 minutes slowly mix in the flour until it thickens. Gently simmer for another 10 minutes, stirring, until yellow fat appears on it. This means it is cooked. You could also stir in an egg while the masovnek is still hot. Serve in a clay dish with sour milk.

KOLINE

The best time for koline is winter, since the meat stays fresh longer. Meat products, which are smoked and cured in fresh cold air will not go off. In Slovenia, meat is usually preserved in salt or cured.

Aspic

6 pork feet, 1kg pork head with ears, 2 pork tongues, soup vegetables (carrots, parsley root, half onion, bay leaf, garlic clove, thick turnip slice, celery, kale leaf), garlic, onion, salt, black pepper, pinch of thyme and marjoram, 1 tablespoon vinegar;

Cook the feet and the head in a large pot. When the meat is half cooked, add the soup vegetables, bay leaf, garlic, salt and black pepper. When the meat is cooked, take it out, leave it to cool and bone it, then chop it into small pieces. Strain the soup and remove the fat. Put the meat in a glass dish and pour the soup over it. You can also add chopped hard boiled eggs and soup vegetables. Leave the aspic in a cold place to harden. When it is hard enough, turn it out of the dish and cut it into small pieces. Mix with chopped onion, vinegar, pumpkin oil and season to taste with salt and pepper.

Grilled Sausages

1,5 kg pork shoulder, 2 mm thin sausage casings, salt, black pepper, crushed garlic soaked in 100 ml of water;

Mince the meat and add the salt, black pepper, and the water and garlic. Mix well and fill the sausage casings. Form sausages and close them with skewers. Cook them briefly in boiling water then roll them in flour and fry them in oil or lard. Serve with sauerkraut or sour turnip.

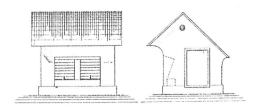

Gorenjsko Sausages with husked millet

2 kg pork, 6 garlic cloves, 200 g husked millet, 100 ml water, salt, black pepper, 2 m of large sausage casings;

Mince the pork. Finely chop the garlic and put it in the water, then pour into the minced pork. Add salt, black pepper and the uncooked millet. Mix well and leave to rest in a cold place. Place the mixture in sausage casings and close with skewers. Each sausage should weigh around 400 g. Do not fill the casings too tightly because the millet expand during cooking. Smoke the sausages with cold smoke. Simmer them gently for 90 minutes. Serve hot or cold.

Zaseka

Meaty pork fat, bay leaf, garlic, salt, pepper corns;

Cut the fat into large pieces, salt it and add the crushed garlic. Use 30 g of salt for every kilogram of pork fat. Put the pieces in a dish and cover them with boiled salted water. Also add some bay leaf and peppercorns. Leave for a few days in a cold place. Next, wipe the pieces and hang them in an airy place to dry well. After that, cure them in cold smoke for few days and then hang them in a cold airy place for another few days. Mince the smoked bacon, season to taste with salt and black pepper, mix in the crushed garlic and put in a container. Melt some lard and pour it on top so that the zaseka doesn't go off. Close the container and store in a cold place.

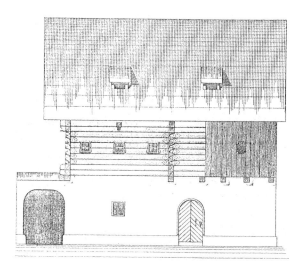

Mežerli

1 kg of pork or veal lungs, 500 g pork or veal heart, 4 tablespoons cracklings (or zaseka), 3 small onions, 750 g white bread, 2 eggs, 300 ml milk, 100 ml sour cream, marjoram, salt, pepper, lard;

Cook the lungs in salted water for 90 minutes, leave them to cool and mince them. Retain the water used for cooking the lungs and heart. Fry the chopped onion in cracklings and pour over the minced lungs. Repeat with the heart. Mix well, add pepper and marjoram. Dice the bread and pour whisked eggs blended with milk and cream over it. Add a ladle of the soup that remains from cooking the lungs and heart. Mix well; if the mixture is too hard, add some more soup. Take a deep clay dish (in the Mežica and Slovenj Gradec area these are known as štecl or pekva) and grease the bottom and the sides, then spread the mixture inside. Bake in the medium hot oven for 45 minutes until a nice yellowish crust is formed. Serve with salad.

Hang washed and dried pieces of meat in the smokehouse for one day without lighting the fire so that the meat dries. After that, use dry beech wood mixed with juniper wood for the fire. The smoke should be warm but not hot. Smoke the meat for a few hours every day and leave it to cool again until it is evenly coloured and dry. Hang the smoked pieces in an airy place until they dry completely.

Koroška White Sausages

1 kg rice, 1 kg pot barley, 2 kg pork lungs, 1/2 pork head, 2 onions, some pork blood, lard, marjoram, basil, salt;

Cook the rice and the pot barley separately till almost done. Rinse with cold water and strain. Cook the lungs and the pork head for about 2 hours or until the meat is easily removed from the bones, leave it to cool and mince. Chop the onion, fry it in lard, add it to the mixture and stir well. If necessary, pour in some of the soup left form cooking the pork head. The mixture should not be too thick because it expands slightly during cooking. Fill washed sausage casing with the mixture and skewer. Cook the sausages for 2 minutes in hot but not boiling water. Take them from the soup, rinse with cold water and leave them to cool on a wooden plate. Serve roasted with bujta repa.

Mavžlji

1 kg pork head, 50 g butter, 1 onion, 150 g white bread, 200 g rice, 4 tablespoons cream, parsley, garlic, marjoram, pimiento, lemon peel, pork membrane;

Clean and cook the pork brain or chop it and fry in some lard. Cook the pork head, bone it and chop the meat. Melt the butter and fry the chopped onion, parsley, bread soaked in milk and crushed garlic in it. Add the milk and the spices and stir into a smooth mixture. Leave it to cool then stir in the brain and the meat.

Cook the rice in the pork soup, cool it and stir it into the mixture. Salt to taste and add some more pork soup if necessary. Wash the membrane, spread it out and cut it into large squares. Put three spoonfuls of the mixture onto each square and wrap it up into mavžlji. Put them into a roasting tin or special clay dish and roast in the oven at 200°C for 40 minutes. Serve hot or cold with sauerkraut and different salads.

Zaseka is prepared in different ways in Slovenia, depending on the region. Usually, the bacon is first smoked and then ground. Zaseka can be served as a seasoning or simply spread on a piece of bread.

Budel

1 cured pork head (2 kg), 2 kg stale white bread, 500 ml milk, 200 ml sour cream, 10 eggs, 1 onion, 5 garlic cloves, parsley, 2 large pieces of pork perotpneum or 2 x 50 cm sausage casing, salt, black pepper, nutmeg;

Dice the bread and soak it in the milk and cream. Beat in an egg and mix well. Cook the pork head and leave it to cool. Bone the head and finely chop the meat. Stir into the bread mixture and season to taste. Add the chopped fried onion, crushed garlic, parsley, salt, black pepper and nutmeg and mix well. Fill the sausage casings with the mixture and close with skewers. You can also shape the mixture into a loaf and wrap it in pork peritoneum. Roast in a medium hot oven for approximately 1 hour. Slice it when it is still warm and serve with horseradish or sauerkraut.

Buckwheat Sausages

500 g cooked pork lungs, 500 g kidneys, 500 g lard, 750 g cooked pork head without bones, 1 kg husked buckwheat, 100 g fried onion, 1 tablespoon marjoram, 100 g salt, 1 teaspoon pimiento, 1.5 litre soup, 6 to 8 m sausage casing;

Cook the pork head with a garlic clove, carrot, bay leaf and 1 onion slice in water then add the buckwheat, half cook and leave to cool. In another pot, cook the lungs and the kidneys. Finely chop all the meat, the kidneys and the lungs. Mix into the buckwheat and season with pimiento, marjoram, black pepper, salt. Pour in melted lard and fried onion and mix well. If the mixture is too thick add some more of the water in which you cooked the meat. Put the mixture into sausage casings and close with skewers. Put the sausages in cold water and heat, ensuring the water does not boil. Take them out of water and leave in a cold room to cool and dry. Roast them in the oven at 190°C for 40 minutes. Serve with potato salad, sauerkraut or sour turnip.

FLOUR BASED DISHES
are served on their own or as side dishes.

Koroška Noodles

Dough: 4 eggs, salt, 400 g flour, parsley, 1 tablespoon apple vinegar, oil;

Stuffing: 1 egg, salt, 300 g dry pears, parsley, 1 slice white bread; 6 tablespoons cracklings for seasoning;

Mix the flour, eggs, salt and vinegar into the dough. If the dough is too dry or too hard, add some water. Divide into two lumps and grease them with oil. Cover with a kitchen cloth and leave in a cold place for 1 hour then roll out the dough until it is as thick as a knife edge. Cut into 10 cm strips and place a teaspoon of stuffing (the size of a hazelnut) every 3 to 5 cm. Mould the dough into a tight roll and squeeze it together between the stuffing balls so that they bulge out. Cut into noodles. Cook the noodles in boiling water for about 15 minutes and season with cracklings. You can also sprinkle them with poppy seed or roughly chopped goats' cheese.

Stuffing: Add 1 egg, white bread (without crust and crumbed) and salt to the finely chopped cooked pears. The stuffing should be compact enough to make small balls. Put in some bread crumbs to thicken it, if necessary. Cherries, cottage cheese, apples or bacon could also be used for the stuffing instead of pears.

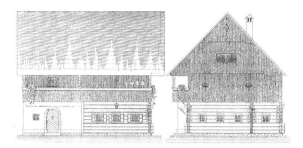

Rateče Squares

Dough: cooked potatoes and flour in the proportion 1/3 potatoes to 2/3 flour (e.g., 200 g peeled cooked potatoes to 400 g flour), salt, 1 egg, margarine;

Stuffing: bread crumbs fried in butter, 500 g cottage cheese, 2 eggs, 200 ml sour cream, salt, chopped tarragon;

Mash the potatoes, add the flour, salt, egg and some margarine. Knead the mixture into a smooth dough. The dough should be harder than that for potato rolls otherwise it tends to fall apart. Divide it into small balls and roll them into squares of up to 12cm. Put a teaspoon of stuffing onto each square, fold them and press firmly together at the top with a fork. Gently boil the squares in salted water for 20 minutes.

Stuffing: Fry the breadcrumbs in some butter and add them to the cottage cheese, eggs, sour cream, fried onion, chopped tarragon, salt. Mix well. The mixture must be fairly compact.

Sprinkle the cooked squares with cracklings or zaseka and serve with sauerkraut or pickled turnips.

Podjuna Obrnenik

500 g plain flour (or 250 g buckwheat flour and 250 g plain flour if you want buckwheat obrnenik), 300 ml cream, 500 ml milk, salt;

Fry the flour in a large pan. In another pan, boil the milk, salt and the cream. When the flour turns golden brown, pour the boiled milk into it and cook for another 10 minutes stirring vigorously until it thickens and does not stick to the bottom of the pan. Form large dumplings and serve with white coffee, milk or sour milk. You can also put the cooked mixture into a dish and leave it to cool then turn it onto a plate and slice it. Alternatively, you could serve it cold with cottage cheese or potato soup.

Ubrnenik

400 g plain flour, 400 ml milk, 250 ml cream, salt;

Fry the flour. Boil the milk with the cream, salt and pour over the fried flour. Mix well. Form small balls and serve them with white coffee or sour milk. For a more sour dish, substitute the cream with sour cream or cottage cheese.

The Gorenjsko Potato Pancake

1 kg potatoes, 1 egg, 100 g flour, salt, 150 ml oil;

Peel the potatoes and grate them. Work in the egg and some salt, then add the flour and mix well. Put some oil into a frying pan and heat it gently. Put in a ladle of the mixture and flatten it with a turner until it is around 10 cm wide and 5 to 10 mm thick. After a few minutes, when it is fried on one side, turn it and let it fry on the other. Serve warm with cottage cheese, or zaseka, or with white coffee.

You could also serve it with stuffing: gently fry some onion, add a chopped garlic clove and cooked sliced soup vegetables then fry for a few minutes and put on the pancakes.

Corn Tomarli

500 g butter, 3 eggs, 4 tablespoons sugar, 750 g corn flour, 100 g white flour, 200 ml white wine, 60 g fresh yeast, 2 cloves, 1 cinnamon stick, grated lemon peel, salt;

Cream the butter, add sugar, eggs and crumbed fresh yeast. (Before fresh yeast was available, people used 'kravajce', made in autumn from corn flour and wine or apple must.) Put in the flour and knead to make a firm smooth dough. If necessary, add a few tablespoons of milk. Spread the dough evenly onto a well greased baking tin or clay dish and leave to rise for another half hour. Bake in the oven at 190°C for some 40 minutes. Cook the wine with the spices. When the dough is cooked, sprinkle it with mulled wine. Cut it up and leave it in the tin to cool. Before serving, sprinkle it with sugar.

There is also the Štajerski Tomerl, which is prepared in the same way except without sugar and spices in the mulled wine. This is served with potato or bean salad.

Gombci

1 kg wheat flour, 50 g fresh yeast, salt and lukewarm water, 200 g cracklings;

Sift the flour into a bowl and remove 5 tablespoons. Crumb the yeast into a small bowl with 10 tablespoons of water and a teaspoon of sugar. Mix well, then add the 5 tablespoons of flour and leave it in a warm place to rise. Make a small hole in the rest of the flour, salt to taste and add the yeast mixture. Sprinkle with lukewarm water and knead to a firm smooth dough. Divide the dough into small fist sized loaves, cover them with a kitchen cloth and leave them to rise until they double in size. Boil some salted water, put in the loaves and simmer them for 15 to 20 minutes in a half-covered pot. When the loaves are cooked, remove them from water and cut them up. Serve in a clay dish with country-style sauerkraut and stuffed pork legs, sprinkled with heated cracklings.

Koroška Grebenci

Dough: 500 g flour, 3 eggs, salt, water;

Stuffing: 750 g dried pears, 150 g rice, 150 g sugar, 2 eggs, 100 g butter, 500 ml milk, 50 g sugar, bread crumbs;

Knead the flour, eggs, lukewarm water and salt into a smooth dough and leave it to rest. Thinly roll out the dough, cut it into 8 x 8 cm squares and put a teaspoon of stuffing onto each of them. Fold the squares together, making ridge-shaped edges. Cook the grebenci in salted water for 15 minutes, strain and sprinkle with breadcrumbs, fried in some butter.

To prepare the stuffing, grind cooked pears and stir in the rice cooked in milk, and the eggs.

Serve with sugar and compote.

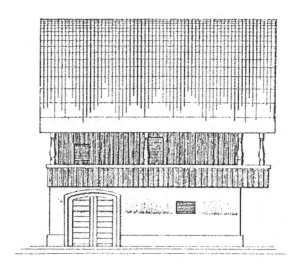

Koroška Buckwheat Žlikrofi

Dough: 500 g flour, 2 eggs, salt, water

Stuffing: 100 g butter, 500 ml cream, 750 kg buckwheat flour;

Knead all ingredients to form a soft dough. Leave it to rest for a while, then roll it out and cut it in 8 x 8 cm large squares. Place the stuffing in walnut sized balls onto these squares.

Stuffing: Bring the cream and butter to the boil, then add the salt and the flour and cook until the mixture leaves the sides of the saucepan, stirring vigorously.

Leave the žlikrofi to cool, then cook for 15 minutes in salted boiling water and sprinkle with breadcrumbs fried in butter. You could also sprinkle them with sugar.

Posolanka

Potato dough: 1 kg potatoes, 2 eggs, 100 ml sour cream, 350 g flour, salt, black pepper, oil, zaseka, garlic;

Cook, peel, mash and cool the potatoes then work in the rest of the ingredients, including the salt and black pepper, to make a smooth dough. Roll it out about 1 cm thick and cut out round pieces. Fry them in hot oil on both sides until golden brown. Take them out and leave on a strainer for a while so that the excess oil drips away. Spread zaseka on them and sprinkle with crushed garlic. Serve with potato salad or sour milk.

Bread Sausages

1 kg bread, 500 g pork head meat, 2.5 litres soup in which you cooked the head, 200 g finely chopped onion, pinch of marjoram and thyme, salt, 200 ml pork blood, pimiento, black pepper;

Cook the meat and add the bread, soaked in soup, fried onion and seasoning. Pour in the soup and the blood and mix well. Stuff the sausage casings with the mixture and make sausages. Cook them for about 10 minutes in hot but not boiling water. When they are done, rinse them with cold water and turn out onto wooden plates. When cold turn them around. Leave them to rest overnight in a cold place.

Kulinji

4 eggs, 500 g wheat flour, 200 ml cream, 100 g lard, poppy seed to sprinkle;

Knead the ingredients into firm dough. Thinly roll out the dough and cut it into squares of 5 x 5 cm. Cook them in salted water and butter them. Serve as a side dish with venison or roast meat. You could also serve them with some cream and sprinkled with poppy seed and sugar.

Chestnut Gnocchi

500 g cooked and peeled chestnuts, 4 eggs, 50 g flour, 100 g butter, 50 g sugar, salt;

Cook and peel the chestnuts, add salt, eggs and flour and knead into a firm dough. Make the gnocchi and fry them in hot butter. Serve on their own sprinkled with sugar or as a side dish.

Buckwheat Šmorn

1 litre milk, 3 eggs, 500 g buckwheat flour, 100 g butter, salt, sugar;

Mix all the ingredients into a smooth, slightly thick batter. Melt the butter in a baking tray and pour the batter into the tray. Bake in the oven at 200°C until it turns golden brown. Take the tin out of the oven and break the batter into small pieces with two forks. Return into the oven and bake for 5 more minutes. Put the šmorn on a plate and sprinkle with sugar. Serve with hot milk, apple puree or cooked prunes. You could also serve it with salad, in which case do not sprinkle with sugar.

Cheese and Potato Salad

750 g potatoes, 500 g cottage cheese, pepper, salt, oil, whey (from the cottage cheese)

Cook the potatoes in their skin, peel them and slice them. Add salt, oil, cottage cheese and whey and shake lightly. Serve with loparnica or on its own with bread.

Cooked Buckwheat Loaf – Vzhajanec

50 g fresh yeast, 500 g buckwheat flour, 500 g white flour, lukewarm water, cracklings (zaseka), salt.

Mix the yeast with some lukewarm water and flour and leave to rise. Then make the dough, cover with a clean kitchen cloth and leave it to rise. Put it on a wooden plate, covered with flour, and form it into a loaf. Cook it in 2 litres of salted water for 45 minutes to 1 hour, then carefully remove it from the water and slice it. Sprinkle with cracklings. Vzhajanec is usually served with meat, sauerkraut, cabbage, turnip and other vegetables, as a main course or with salad. It also goes well with cottage cheese.

Bean Mash

750 g beans, 750 g sauerkraut, bay leaf, salt, lard, 3 garlic cloves, 1 kg potatoes;

Cook the beans with the bay leaf and garlic in salted water until tender. In another pot, cook peeled sliced potatoes, strain them and sprinkle with butter. You can also add some sour cream. Put the beans and the potatoes together and mash them. Add the crushed garlic fried in cracklings. Serve with sauerkraut and grilled sausage, black pudding or cured ribs.

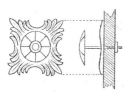

Gorenjsko Stuffed Triangles

Dough: 500 g buckwheat flour, 100 g white flour, 500 ml boiling water, salt, 30 g butter or lard;

Stuffing: 150 g cottage cheese, 200 ml sour cream, 1 egg, 30 g bread crumbs, salt;

Scald the buckwheat flour with salted boiling water, knead the ingredients into a dough and cover with a kitchen cloth. Leave it to cool. When cold, work in the white flour and leave it to rest. Roll out the dough (about 5 mm thick) and cut it into squares. Mix together the cottage cheese, sour cream, 1 egg, breadcrumbs and salt to make the stuffing. Put a teaspoon of stuffing onto each square. Fold them into triangles and press the edges firmly together. Cook them in salted water for 15 minutes, then strain them and sprinkle them with fried breadcrumbs.

KAŠE, ŽGANCI

used to form the staple diet of the Slovene farmer. They can be served on their own or as a side dish.

Rašovna

750 g husked millet, 500 g pickled turnip, 4 tablespoons cracklings, 1 onion, 3 crushed garlic cloves, cumin, marjoram, black peppercorns, bay leaf;

Cook the turnip with the herbs for about 1 hour. When it is half-cooked add the millet and let it simmer for 30 more minutes until the turnip is cooked. Finely chop the onion and fry it with the garlic in cracklings or zaseka until golden brown and add to the cooked turnip. Mix well and let it simmer for another 5 minutes. Serve with boiled potatoes.

Mixed Corn Žganci

500 g corn groats, 500 g corn flour, salt, boiling water, 150 g cracklings or zaseka

Mix together the corn flour and the groats and heat the mixture up in a saucepan, stirring it for about 5 minutes, ensuring that the mixture does not change colour. Pour in salted boiling water until the žganci can be easily crumbled with a fork. Sprinkle with heated cracklings or zaseka.

George's Hat

500 g buckwheat flour, 4 eggs, 100 g zaseka or lard with cracklings, 500 ml sour milk, salt;

Cook the buckwheat flour in salted boiling water for 5 minutes then make a hole into the pile. Cook the žganci for another 20 minutes. Remove half of the liquid – žgančevka – and keep it in case the žganci turn out too dry. Crumble the žganci with a fork and mix in the melted zaseka. Put them in a bowl and cover with an egg omelette so they have a 'hat'. You could also pour in the sour milk.

Staircase millet

500 g husked millet, a small onion, 100 g lard with cracklings, 30 g flour, salt;

Clean and soak the millet then cook it until thick. Chop the onion and fry it in lard together with a tablespoon of flour until golden brown. Pour the roux into the cooked millet. Cook for a few more minutes, then put it into a bowl in a cone-like shape. Make several 'stairs' into the cone. Melt the lard with cracklings and pour it over the cone so that the lard and the cracklings stay on the 'stairs'. Serve as a main dish with baked potatoes.

Prune millet

500 g husked millet, 1 litre milk, 100 g prunes, 100 g sugar, ground cinnamon, 100 g butter;

Wash the millet and soak it overnight, then put it in boiling milk and cook. When it is half cooked, add the washed prunes, sugar and cinnamon. Serve in a clay dish buttered with melted butter and sprinkled with sugar (to taste).

Corn žganci, buckwheat žganci and millet groats with prunes used to be the staple diet for simple farmers.

The Hole

400 ml husked millet, 6 tablespoons butter, 800 ml milk, cinnamon, salt;

Wash the millet and cook it in salted milk for 20 to 25 minutes stirring constantly. Turn it out into a pile on top of which you make a hole with a wooden spoon. Melt the butter and pour it into the hole. Sprinkle with cinnamon and sugar.

George's Hat is a typical dish enjoyed by the woodcutters and charcoal-burners in the Alpine region of Slovenia.

MEAT DISHES
**used to be served on festive occasions or on Sundays,
when the whole family gathered at the dinner table.**

Tržič Roast Beef
For 8 to 10 people: 1.5 kg beef, preferably leg or loin, cut into smaller pieces of about 150 g each, about 7 kg of onions, calamint, juniper berries, bay leaf, garlic, 2 kg potatoes, salt, black pepper, stock;

Wash the meat and scald until it loses its smell. Heat the lard in a large pot and add the chopped onions. Use a kilo of onions per kilo of meat. Fry for a few minutes then add the meat. Cover with a lid and simmer for about 1 hour. Add the calamint and juniper berries. In Tržič they say that the roast beef should be coloured by the calamint. Put in the bay leaf, crushed garlic, black pepper and salt. Simmer for another 1/2 hour till the onions dissolve. When the meat is tender, sprinkle with flour, stir and pour in the hot soup. Simmer for another 15 minutes, then add 10 medium-sized, half-cooked, peeled potatoes. Cook until the potatoes are soft. The dish should be thicker than chicken stew but thinner than goulash.

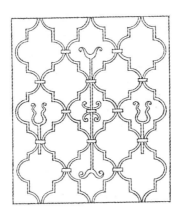

St. Martin's Goose
1 goose, salt, pepper, marjoram, caraway seed, 5 apples, 200 g chestnuts, 6 shallots, 30 g lard, 25 ml grape brandy, 100 ml wine;

Clean and wash the goose then rub it with salt on the outside and with salt, pepper, marjoram and crushed caraway seed on the inside. Fill it with sliced apples, cooked and peeled chestnuts and shallots which you have briefly fried in some lard. Sew up the hole, put the goose into a pan on its back, add 100 ml of wine and roast in the oven at 210°C for 90 minutes. Turn it around a few times during that time, basting it occasionally, so that a light brown crust is

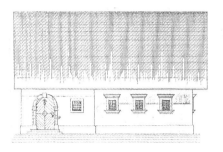 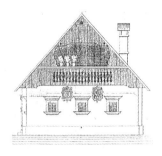

formed. Cover it with brandy a few minutes before it is done. When the goose has a nice brownish crust, put it in another dish and remove the grease from the pan. Add the drippings and bring to the boil. Pour the mixture on the goose and serve with mlinci, bread dumplings, roast potatoes, cauliflower, red cabbage or cabbage salad.

Kvinta – Roast Duck

1 young duck, salt, lard

Stuffing Suggestions:

Stuffing 1: chopped duck liver, 200 g bread, 200 ml white wine, 3 eggs, 50 g breadcrumbs, 100 g sheep's milk cheese, 1 onion, pinch of salt, pepper, coriander, celery and calamint;

Stuffing 2: 500 g cooked peeled chestnuts, 100 g chopped bacon, 200 ml white wine, salt, pinch of pepper and rosemary;

Stuffing 3: same as for Stuffing 2 and 500 g grated apples;

Clean the duck and rub it well with salt on the outside and on the inside. Fill it with one of the suggested stuffings, sew it up and roast it in the oven at 210°C for approximately 2 hours. For Stuffing 1, soak the bread in white wine, cook the eggs and grate them, then add chopped liver, bread crumbs, grated cheese, all the seasoning and mix well. For Stuffing 2 cook, peel and mash the chestnuts, add the chopped bacon, wine and the seasoning and mix well.

The name for this dish originates from the fact that traditionally 100 day old ducks (kvinta comes from the Latin word for hundred) are meant to be the best for roasting.

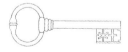

Bela Krajina Fried Mincemeat

800 g pork, salt, pepper, garlic;

Batter: 200 ml milk, 2 eggs, 150 g flour, salt;

Mix the milk, egg yolks and the flour into a batter slightly thicker than that for pancakes. Whisk the egg whites until stiff and fold them into the batter. Mince the meat, add pepper, salt and crushed garlic and mix well. Divide the mixture into 10 small loafs. First roll them in flour, then in the batter and fry in hot oil for 5 minutes on each side.

Vine Leaf Sarma

20 fresh vine leaves (medium sized), 1 kg chicken, 200 g bacon, 40 g onion, 50 g lard, 250 g rice, 3 garlic cloves, parsley, celery, salt, pepper, bay leaf, marjoram, calamint, 2 eggs, 5 tablespoons oil, 80 g flour, 50 g onion, 1 kg tomatoes (ripe), 1/2 litre sour cream;

Blanche the vine leaves, divide them and cut out the veins. Fry finely chopped onions in lard until golden brown. Mince the chicken (without the skin and bones) with bacon and fry it together with the onion. Leave it to cool, then add the seasoning, crushed garlic, salt, cooked rice (cook it for 3/4 of the usual cooking time), eggs and mix well.

Put some of the prepared mixture on each vine leaf, roll them up and push the ends inside. Arrange the rolls into a cooking pot, fill it with water so that 3/4 of the rolls are covered and simmer them, half covered with a lid, for 45 minutes until tender.

To make the sauce from the tomatoes first boil them in some water for 5 minutes, then take them out and put them in cold water. Leave to cool, peel and halve them. Remove the seeds, mix well in a blender, add the sauce to the rolls and boil gently for another 15 minutes. Finally, blend in the sour cream and serve.

Corn žganci goes well with sour milk or as a side dish with sauerkraut or sour turnip.

Lukarsko meso

600 g pork fillet, 300 g carrots, 50 g parsley root, 2 bay leaves, 10 black peppercorns, 50 g capers, 2 gherkins, 1 small lemon, 300 g onion, 20 g paprika, 2 tomatoes, 100 ml oil, salt, 200 ml white wine;

Put some water in a pot, add salt and sliced carrots, parsley root, bay leaf and one half of a large onion which you have partly fried on a hot plate. Divide the herbs in half. Add one half to the water and cook for 10 minutes. Put in the pork fillet and cook for another 5 minutes. Remove from the heat and leave to cool.

Slice the rest of the onion and fry it in oil. Add cooked sliced carrots and parsley from the soup, them put in the paprika, bay leaf, capers, peeled chopped lemon, grated gherkins and chopped tomatoes. Fry for 10 minutes, pour in the white wine and simmer for another 5 minutes. Put the meat into another dish and cover it with the marinade. Leave it in a cool place for a day. Before serving, slice the fillet, then serve with marinade and home-made corn bread.

Carniola-Style Chicken

1 chicken, 150 g veal liver, 100 g chicken liver, 150 g veal, 150 g bacon, 150 g fresh mushrooms – boletus or 30 g dried boletus soaked in water, 2 slices white bread soaked in milk, 2 cooked potatoes, 1 egg, 1 onion, garlic, parsley, calamint, rosemary, black pepper, 20 thin slices bacon;

Mince the veal, veal liver, chicken liver, soaked bread and bacon in a food processor. Add the eggs, fried chopped onion, garlic, salt, black pepper, rosemary, parsley, some calamint and chopped mushrooms to the mixture. Mix well. Cut the potatoes into slices of about 1.5 cm and fry them on both sides until golden brown. Clean and thoroughly wash the chicken. Place the potato slices evenly inside the chicken, then add the mixture. Close the hole with toothpicks. Wrap the chicken with sliced bacon and tie it with a string. Put it into an ovenproof dish and pour hot oil over it. Roast it in the oven at 180°C for 2 hours and baste it. When it is nearly done, pour over 200 ml of white wine.

Veal Terrine

Ingredients for a clay dish with lid: 300 g veal filet, 200 g lean pork, 400 g bacon, 1 teaspoon salt, 1/2 teaspoons of dried green pepper, basil, sage and thyme, 50 g white bread without crust, 1 egg white, 6 tablespoons cream, 30 g butter, 2 shallots, 200 g veal liver, 2 cl Cognac, 2 cl Cointreau, 1/2 teaspoon salt, 1 garlic clove, a pinch of ground ginger or cardamom, 125 ml cream, 200 g button mushrooms, 2 tablespoons chopped parsley, 120 g cooked ham, 250 g sliced bacon;

Slice the meat and 400 g of bacon into slices of about 1 cm. Put them in a bowl and season with salt and herbs. Slice the bread and put the slices on the meat. Mix the egg white with cream and pour over the bread. Cover with tin foil and leave in a cold place for 12 hours. To prepare the mixture for the terrine, called 'farce', all the ingredients must be cold. Mince the marinated meat and bacon twice, put it in a bowl with ice around it, add the marinated bread and stir until the mixture becomes shiny, slowly pouring in the cream. Fry the mushrooms and leave them to cool. Chop the ham and mix in together with the mushrooms.

Take the rest of the bacon and line the inside of the clay dish with it. Put in the mixture with some bacon strips and cover with the remaining bacon. Cover with a lid. Cook the terrine in a water bath in the oven at 200°C or in a convection oven at 190°C for 50 minutes. The water must not get hotter than 80 °C and it should come up to two fingers below the top of the dish.

Rabbit With Mlinci

1 rabbit (about 2 kg), 20 thin slices smoked bacon, 1 small onion, 1 small celery root, 3 carrots, 2 tablespoons lard, 100 ml white or red wine, salt, pepper, 1 teaspoon mustard, 100 ml sour cream;

Wash the rabbit and remove the skin and the veins, then cut into its back and remove the thigh bone. Coat it with mustard, sprinkle with ground black pepper, cover with smoked bacon and put it into a greased ovenproof dish. Add the finely chopped onion, carrots, celery and white or red wine. Roast it in the oven at 200°C for up to 1 1/2 hours, basting it several times. Cut the roasted rabbit into large pieces, then arrange them on a plate so that they resemble the original shape of the rabbit. Press the vegetables through a strainer, add 100 ml of cream and bring to the boil. Pour the sauce over the rabbit and serve it with cranberries and mlinci (or porridge rolls).

Turkey with Mlinci

1 young turkey, 1 litre fowl soup, 150 g lard, 500 g mlinci

Clean and wash the turkey. Rub it with salt and cover it with lard. While it is roasting keep basting it water or soup so you also get the sauce for the mlinci. Just before it is done, crush the mlinci, scald them with hot water and leave for a few minutes, then add to the turkey. Roast until the turkey and the mlinci have a nice golden crust. Cut the turkey into pieces and put the mlinci around it. Serve with salad.

Prekmurje-Style Partridge

1 partridge, 50 g thinly sliced smoked bacon, 1 onion, 200 ml chicken soup, garlic, cumin, parsley, sweet red paprika, 20 g flour, 200 ml sour cream, mlinci, cracklings;

Soak the partridge for 3 days in a mixture made of soup vegetables (carrots, parsley root, a slice of root celery, 1 onion, 1 garlic clove) and some juniper berries. After this time, wrap the partridge in bacon and tie with a string. Pour hot oil over it and roast it in the oven for 40 minutes at 190°C in a covered roasting dish. Just before it is done, add the diced bacon, chopped onion and a tablespoon of flour into the roasting dish. Cover again and roast for another 15 minutes until tender. Put the partridge on a plate, then add the chicken soup into the roasting dish and simmer for a few minutes. Stir in the sour cream and pour the sauce over the partridges. Serve with mlinci sprinkled with cracklings.

Sunday Mulprata

900 g beef tenderloin, 6 tomatoes, cleaned out and smothered in butter, 300 g onion puree, 6 meat žličniki (made with veal), 2 boletus, 6 smothered lettuce halves, 100 ml red wine;

Quickly fry the tenderloin in lard and then smother it for about 20 minutes. Take it out of the pan and keep it warm. Stir the wine into the remaining sauce, add some beef soup if necessary and bring to the boil. Mix in some starch flour, simmer for a few more minutes, pass through a sieve and serve in a tureen. Slice the tenderloin, put the slices on an oval wooden plate and put the lettuce and the tomatoes, stuffed with onion puree, around it to get a nice colour contrast. Add meat žličniki at both ends of the plate. Slice and fry the boletus and put them on the tenderloin slices.

Trieste-style Tripe

1 kg cooked tripe, 1.5 litres beef soup, 100 ml oil, 150 g bacon, 1 big onion, few garlic cloves, 1 tablespoon tomato puree, 1 tablespoon sweet paprika, 60 g bread crumbs, beef soup, salt, black pepper, bay leaf, parsley sprigs, parmesan;

Cut the cooked tripe into strips. Finely chop the onion and fry it in oil together with the chopped bacon and breadcrumbs. Before it turns yellow, add the tomato puree and tripe. Mix and smother briefly. Stir in the ground paprika, crushed garlic, chopped parsley, salt, black pepper and some beef soup. Gently simmer the tripe for approximately 1 hour. The dish should be thick. Serve sprinkled with parmesan.

Stuffed Smoked Pork Leg

4 medium-sized smoked pork legs, 200 g cooked husked millet, 1/2 onion, 4 garlic cloves, 2 eggs, 4 carrots (small), 1 bunch celery and parsley, thyme, rosemary, calamint, ground black pepper;

Cook the pork legs with clean, washed carrots for about 1 hour, depending on their size, and when the legs are cooked, remove the bones. Retain the water in which they were cooking. In the meantime, prepare the stuffing: mix together the cooked porridge oats, spices, eggs, fried onion, garlic and celery. Fill the legs with the stuffing and carrots cut into strips, close and tie them with a string. Return them into the water in which they were previously cooking, bring to the boil, then lower the heat and simmer for 10 minutes. Serve them cut into thick slices with sauerkraut and mushrooms.

Budlan Tongue

1 beef tongue, 2 eggs, 80 g butter, 60 g bread crumbs, few parsley sprigs, 1 half onion, black pepper, salt;

Cook the tongue in salted water until tender. Cut the fat end of the tongue off and chop it finely. Mix in two eggs, 50 g butter, 30 g breadcrumbs, finely chopped parsley and onion, black pepper and salt. Cut the tongue along one side to get a small pocket which you fill with the prepared mixture. Close the opening with toothpicks or sew it together. Spread the tongue with beaten egg, sprinkle it with the remaining breadcrumbs, pour boiling butter over it and roast in the oven at 190°C until the upper side is golden brown.

Dolenjsko Balls

250 g beef leg joint, 250 g veal shoulder, 250 g pork neck, 2 slices white bread, some milk to soak the bread, 50 g onion, 1 garlic clove, 1 egg, salt, black pepper, 20 g flour;

Batter: 100 ml milk, pinch of salt, 2 egg yolks, 100 g flour, 1 egg white, frying oil;

Make the batter at least 1 hour in advance and leave it to rest. Mince all three kinds of meat, soak the bread in milk, squeeze out the milk and add the bread to the meat. Finely chop and fry the onion and add to the meat together with the egg yolk, crushed garlic, seasoning and flour. Mix well and divide the mixture into medium sized balls. First, roll the balls in flour and then in batter, and deep fry them. The oil in which you fry them should not be too hot. Serve the fried balls with potato or tomato salad on their own for lunch.

Žlikrofi with Bakalca Sauce

Dough: 500 g flour, 3 eggs, 100 ml lukewarm water, salt;

Stuffing: 1 kg potatoes, 100 g smoked bacon, 50 g oil, 120 g onion, marjoram, black pepper, salt, chives;

Bakalca: 1 kg mutton, 100 g lard or oil, 250 g chopped onion, 200 g grated carrots, 1 tablespoon sour cream, some bone soup, wine, salt, black pepper, bay leaf, calamint and thyme;

Knead the flour, the eggs and some lukewarm water into a dough, softer than that for noodles. Leave it to rest for 20 minutes. Prepare the stuffing. Cook, peel and mash the potatoes. Chop and fry the onion in lard or oil together with the herbs and seasoning. Add to the potatoes and mix well. Divide the mixture into walnut-sized balls. Thinly roll out the dough into a rectangular shape. Put the stuffing balls on half of the dough in lines some 2 cm apart. Cover with the other half of the dough and press firmly between the stuffing. Cut along pressed lines

Carniolan sausage is one of the best known sausages in Slovenia. It is made from the best parts of pork. To make carniolan sausages, take 2/3 of lean and 1/3 of fat meat from the leg joint and shoulder. Per every kilogram take 30 g of salt and 1g saltpetre (if there is too much saltpetre the sausages are too dry and hard), 1 g of roughly crushed black pepper and garlic to taste. Cut the meat into small pieces, add the seasoning and add some white wine in which you have soaked crushed garlic. Grind the mixture and mix well once again. Fill the sausage casings. Hang the sausages for 3 days in cold smoke. In Štajerska they also add some ground cumin to the mixture.

to get žlikrofi with small ears which resemble ravioli. Put them in boiling water. When they rise to the top, they are done. Serve on their own, sprinkled with cracklings, or alternatively with bakalca sauce.

To make bakalca, fry the onion in lard or oil, add the carrots and diced meat. Pour in some bone soup, season to taste, add the white wine and smother. When the meat is tender, sprinkle with flour, fry briefly, add the soup and bring to the boil. When it has reached the boil, stir in a tablespoon of sour cream.

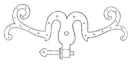

FISH

Salmon in Caper Sauce

1 salmon, cut into slices, lemon juice, 200 ml water, 200 ml white wine, 1 tablespoon vinegar, salt, onion, 4 pepper corns, 4 pimiento corns, 1 tablespoon butter, 1 tablespoon flour, 1 tablespoon capers, a pinch of salt and sugar, 1 egg yolk, 1/2 lemon;

Briefly rinse the salmon slices, dry them, sprinkle with lemon juice and leave them for 10 minutes. Put the water, the wine, vinegar, salt, peeled onion, pepper and pimiento corns and bay leaf into a large saucepan, bring to the boil and cook for 5 minutes. Add the salmon slices and cook for 15 minutes. Take them out and arrange them on a hot plate. Pass the remaining liquid through a strainer. Melt the butter in a saucepan, add the flour and fry it until golden brown, then pour in the liquid, stirring constantly. Bring to the boil, add capers, salt and sugar. Mix together the egg yolk and the cream with 1 tablespoon of hot sauce. Remove the saucepan from the heat and thicken the sauce with the egg mixture. Pour over the salmon slices and decorate with lemon slices and parsley sprigs.

Pierced Trout

1 trout of around 2 kg, 250 g sliced bacon, 2 tins anchovies, 6 potatoes, 500 ml sour cream, 200 g butter, 15 garlic cloves, 200 ml white wine, salt, black pepper;

Clean and wash the fish. Rub it with salt. Place bacon stripes and anchovies inside it across its back and tail. Cut the garlic cloves in half and stick them in the dish. Peel the potatoes and put them inside the fish. Put the fish on a roasting tray and pour boiling butter over it. Roast it in the oven at 190°C for 45 minutes, occasionally pouring the sauce from the tin over it. After 35 minutes cover it generously with sour cream. When finished, put it on a serving tray and pour the wine into the tin. Simmer for a few more minutes. Pour the sauce over the fish. Serve with toast and potato salad.

Fish Fillets on Rice

8 fillets of 100 g each, 200 g long grain unpolished rice, 500 ml water, 1 vegetable stock cube, 500 g cucumbers or zucchinis, 2 pinches freshly ground white pepper, 200 ml cream, 3 tablespoons lemon juice, 1 egg, 2 tablespoons chopped fresh dill, 1 lemon, 1 tomato;

Dissolve the vegetable stock cube in the water in a large pan, add the rice and gently simmer for 15 minutes. Dice the cucumbers or the zucchinis and spread them evenly on the rice. Season with pepper. Cover with a lid and simmer for another 15 minutes. Beat the cream with 2 tablespoons of lemon juice, egg and 1 tablespoon of chopped dill. Wash the fillets, season them with remaining pepper and put them on top of the cucumbers or zucchinis. Pour over the cream mixture and simmer very gently for 10 more minutes. Remove from the heat. Sprinkle the dish with the rest of chopped dill and lemon juice. Decorate with lemon and tomato slices.

Farm-style Char

4 chars (about 250 g each), 4 tablespoons lemon juice, 150 g bacon, 2 onions, 1 bunch parsley, freshly ground white pepper, salt, 2 tablespoons corn flour;

Gut and wash the chars. Sprinkle them with lemon juice and leave them for 10 minutes. Finely chop the bacon. Peel the onions and slice them in rings. Chop the parsley. Fry the bacon in a saucepan until lightly browned, then remove it from the pan and keep it warm. Put the onion rings in the same saucepan and fry them lightly in the remaining oil, then take them out and keep them warm with the bacon. Season the fish with salt and white pepper, and roll them in corn flour. Gently fry them in the saucepan, take them out and keep them warm. Return the bacon and the onion to the saucepan, add the chopped parsley and reheat. Sprinkle on the fish. Serve with potato salad and a slice of lemon.

Roast Trout

1 gutted trout (about 1,5 kg), juice of 1 lemon, 3 slices white bread, 10 garlic cloves, 1 bunch parsley, 1 tablespoon paprika, salt, pepper, 100 ml olive oil;

Wash the fish and sprinkle it with lemon juice and salt both on the inside and outside. Cut the crust off the bread slices and finely crumb the soft part. Chop the parsley and the garlic. Stuff the fish with half of the mixture of parsley and garlic. Mix the remaining half with paprika, bread and olive oil and spread on the fish. Grease a large piece of tin foil, wrap the fish in it and roast in hot oven for 40 minutes. At the same time, roast some potatoes seasoned with thyme and bay-leaf. Serve in the tin foil with lemon slices.

Chars with Bacon

4 gutted chars of 200 g each, juice of 1 lemon, 200 ml soup, 600 g cottage cheese, 1 egg, 100 g bacon, thinly sliced, 2 shallots, 1 tablespoon butter, 2 garlic cloves, parsley, rosemary, corn flour, some soup;

Rub the chars with lemon juice and salt. Finely chop the garlic, parsley and the shallots. Mix the cottage cheese with the egg, garlic and parsley and season with salt and pepper. Stuff the fish with the mixture, then roll them in corn flour, wrap with the slices of bacon and put them in a large ovenproof dish, generously greased with olive oil. Roast in a medium hot oven for 25 minutes. Melt the butter in a saucepan, put in the shallots and fry until golden brown. Pour in the soup, leave it to simmer for a while, then pour over the fish and roast for another 10 minutes. Serve with cabbage salad and potatoes.

Shepherd-Style Fried Char

4 gutted chars, 250 ml milk, 150 g plain flour, 100 g butter, 100 ml oil, grated cheese;1 lemon, salt, pepper, parsley;

Wash the chars and sprinkle them with salt. Roll them in flour, then in milk and again in flour. Heat the oil and the butter in a saucepan and fry the trout until crispy. Take them out and briefly wrap in paper napkins to remove the excess oil. Put them on a plate and sprinkle with grated cheese and a mixture of chopped parsley, pepper and oil, and with diced lemon (without the peel). Serve with fried potato slices.

ŠTRUKLJI, ROLLS, DUMPLINGS, GIBANICA
are just a few dishes which are representative
of the rich variety of Slovenian cuisine.

Loparnica

500 g spinach, 500 g carrots, 500 g cabbage, 750 g onions, 5 garlic cloves, 250g margarine, 500 g cottage cheese, breadcrumbs
Herbs: bay leaf, caraway seed, ground pepper, thyme, sage, marjoram, nutmeg, salt, 100 – 200 ml oil, 3 eggs, 25 ml sour cream, parsley, chopped celery.
2 packets of 500 g ready-made dough

Finely chop the onions then divide into 3 equal portions. Fry each portion in a separate saucepan until cooked but not coloured. Wash the vegetables. In the first saucepan put the spinach, in the second, grated carrots, and in the third scalded cabbage. Equally distribute the herbs and salt into the pots. Cook until tender, then remove from the stove and leave to cool slightly.

Grease a baking tin with margarine. Put in the dough, then a layer of cottage cheese, another layer of dough, then a layer of carrots and again the dough, another layer of spinach and the dough, and finally a layer of cabbage. Cover with a layer of dough. Then repeat, adding a few tablespoons of the egg and sour cream mixture between each layer. Put it in a preheated oven and bake it at 180°C for 1 !/2 hours. While in the oven occasionally pour in a mixture of sour cream and milk.

Buckwheat Squares

Dough: 500 g buckwheat flour, 50 g butter, 1 egg, water, salt, breadcrumbs;
Stuffing: 150 g butter, 400 g buckwheat flour, 250 ml sour cream, salt;

Knead the flour, eggs, water and salt into a pasta dough and leave it to rest. To prepare the stuffing, boil the sour cream and butter, add the buckwheat flour and salt. Cook until the mixture stops sticking to the wooden spoon, stirring constantly.

Thinly roll out the dough (make it as thick as the knife edge). Cut it into 8 x 8 cm squares, put a teaspoon of stuffing on half of them and cover them with the other half of squares. Squeeze them together tightly along the edges. Cook them in salted water for approximately 20 minutes then take them out and serve sprinkled with breadcrumbs fried in butter.

Dolenjska Štruklji

Pastry: 500 g flour, 2 teaspoons oil, 2 eggs, 1 tablespoon apple vinegar, lukewarm water;
Stuffing: 150 g lard, 300 g breadcrumbs, 5 eggs, 500 ml warm double cream, salt, black pepper;

Make the pastry from the necessary ingredients, divide it into 3 pieces, coat each one with oil and leave them to rest for about 1 hour. Thinly roll out the pastry on a floured cloth. Coat it with cream and sprinkle with fried breadcrumbs and scrambled eggs. Roll the štruklji with the help of the cloth and put the roll on a wet kitchen cloth sprinkled with breadcrumbs. Wrap up and tie with a string. Cook the tightly rolled štruklji in salted water for half an hour. When finished, take it out, unwrap it, slice it, sprinkle with cracklings or serve with žejnof – a special kind of homemade mustard, prepared in Dolenjsko from wine must and mustard seed.

Cottage cheese štruklji is a very filling dish.

Cottage Cheese Štruklji

Pastry: 240 ml flour, 125 ml lukewarm water, 1 tablespoon oil, salt, 1 egg;
Stuffing: 500 g cottage cheese, 2 eggs, 250 ml sour cream, 1 tablespoon chopped parsley, 1 tablespoon white breadcrumbs, 1 tablespoon butter, salt;

To prepare the stuffing, put the cottage cheese in a strainer and leave it for a while so the liquid drips away. Next, crumble the cottage cheese with a fork and work in the egg yolks, sour cream and firmly whisked egg whites. Season with salt. Sift the flour into a bowl and make a small hole in it, add the salt and oil and slowly pour in the lukewarm water. Knead to make a smooth pastry (the exact amount of water depends on the dryness of the flour). Put the dough on a

The differences between the regions in Slovenia are also reflected in the country's sausages. Sausages can be made from various ingredients like porridge, pot barley or just from skin, liver or some blood.

floured plate and cover it with a warmed bowl. To make cooked štruklji, work 1 egg or just an egg white into the pastry at the same time as you put in the salt and the oil. The pastry will roll better if you knead in a few tablespoons of sour milk. Leave the pastry to rest for at least half an hour then roll it out very thinly on a floured table cloth, ensuring it doesn't get torn. Cut off the thickest edges. Melt the butter in a saucepan and fry chopped parsley in it. Spread that evenly on the pastry, sprinkle with breadcrumbs, spread on the stuffing and roll tightly with the help of the cloth. Put on a wet kitchen cloth sprinkled with breadcrumbs, wrap it up and tie at both ends. You could also use buttered tin foil instead of the wet kitchen cloth. Cook it in salted water for 20 minutes. Take it out, put it on a wooden plate, unwrap it and cut into 3 cm wide slices. Serve with a main dish and salad of your choice.

Word of advice: Don't salt the pastry while you make it but before you spread on the stuffing so it rolls better.

You can also make štruklji with potato dough; the cooking process is the same as for the pastry for cottage cheese štruklji.

Cottage Cheese Štruklji with Potato Dough

Potato dough: 750 g mashed potatoes, 80 g butter, 2 egg yolks, 1-2 tablespoons salt, yeast mixture made of 40 g fresh yeast, 1 tablespoon sour cream, 300 g flour, nutmeg, 1 tablespoon chopped parsley or chives;

Stuffing: same as for the cottage cheese štruklji

Knead the mashed potatoes, flour, butter, salt, yeast mixture, egg yolks, parsley, nutmeg and sour cream to make a smooth dough. Leave it to rest for at least half an hour. Roll it out on a floured table cloth about 5 mm thick, spread the stuffing on it and roll tightly with the help of the tablecloth. Cover it with a cloth and leave it to rise in a warm place, then roll it in a wet kitchen cloth, sprinkled with breadcrumbs or in buttered tin foil. Cook in salted water for twenty minutes. When finished, unwrap it, cut it into 4 cm wide slices and serve. You could also bake the štruklji. Put it in a greased baking tin and coat with the beaten eggs which you have omitted in preparing the dough. Bake it and serve.

Prlekija Gibanica

Pastry: 350 g flour, 1 tablespoon oil, salt, lukewarm water;

Stuffing: 800 g cottage cheese, 300 ml sour cream, 100 g raisins, 200 g sugar, 3 eggs, grated lemon peel, vanilla sugar, rum;

Knead the ingredients into a smooth pastry and divide it into 4 small lumps. Grease a baking tin. Prepare the stuffing from the cottage cheese, half of the sour cream, raisins, 2 eggs, sugar, lemon peel, vanilla sugar and rum. In another bowl, mix together the rest of the sour cream, the remaining eggs and some sugar. Thinly roll out the first lump, put it in the baking tin, cut off the edges and spread on the stuffing. Repeat the procedure 3 times. Finish with the pastry and pour over the sour cream mixture. Bake in the oven at 180°C for about 45 minutes.

Cottage Cheese Dumplings

300 g cottage cheese, 80 g butter, 2 eggs, 2 egg yolks, 70 g wheat porridge oats, 120 g flour;

Put the butter and the egg yolks into a bowl and mix until creamy. Add the cottage cheese, eggs, porridge and flour. Make a smooth mixture and divide it into dumplings about 4 cm wide. Cook them in salted boiling water for 20 minutes. Before serving, sprinkle them with fried breadcrumbs. Serve as a side dish with meat or on their own with lettuce.

Cottage Cheese Štruklji in Buckwheat Pastry

Pastry: 750 g buckwheat flour, salt, 1 litre boiling water, some white flour;

Stuffing: 2 bunches peppermint, 1 kg cottage cheese, 3 eggs, 5 tablespoons cream, breadcrumbs, 50 g butter and breadcrumbs to sprinkle the štruklji;

To prepare the stuffing, mix together the cottage cheese, eggs, cream and chopped peppermint.

Scald the buckwheat flour with boiling water, mix well and leave it to cool. Put it on a floured surface, knead it and roll it out about 1 cm thick. Spread on the stuffing, sprinkle with breadcrumbs, especially if the stuffing is watery, and roll tightly. Roll the štrukelj in a wet kitchen cloth sprinkled with breadcrumbs and cook it in salted water for 30 minutes. While it is cooking fry some breadcrumbs in butter or melt some cracklings. When the štrukelj is cooked, take it out, unwrap it, slice it, put the slices into a bowl or on a plate and sprinkle with fried breadcrumbs or melted cracklings. If you wish, you can also sprinkle it with sugar.

Kozjansko Parcels

Dough: 250 g buckwheat flour, 250 g flour, 2 eggs;

Stuffing: 100 g husked millet, 300 g cottage cheese, 1 egg, 1 egg yolk, salt, sour cream, cracklings;

Scald the buckwheat flour with hot water, add the white flour and the eggs and knead into a firm dough. To prepare the stuffing, cook the millet, strain it and leave it to cool. Add the cottage cheese, some salt, the egg and the egg yolk. Mix well. Thinly roll out the dough and cut it into pieces of 8 x 8 cm. Put a tablespoon of stuffing on each piece and wrap up the pieces, making small parcels. Press the edges firmly together. Cook them in salted water for 20 minutes, sprinkle with hot cracklings and sour cream.

Krapči

Dough: 600 g flour, 40 g fresh yeast, salt, 100 g lard, 500 ml milk, 50 g sugar, 1 egg yolk;

Stuffing: 400 g cottage cheese, 500 ml milk, 100 g husked millet, 50 g sugar, 200 ml sour cream, 1 egg ;

To prepare the stuffing, boil the milk, salt it and cook the millet in it. Leave to cool then mix in the cottage cheese, cream, sugar and the egg.

Knead the rest of the ingredients into a smooth leavened dough and leave in a warm place until it doubles in size. Roll it out very thinly on a table cloth and spread on the stuffing. Roll it up with table cloth and put into a greased roasting tray. Leave it to rise again in a warm place, brush with beaten egg and bake in the oven at 180°C for about 45 minutes.

Kobansko Gibanica – "Loparošnica"

Dough: 500 g flour, 30 g yeast, 3 tablespoons sugar, 3 egg yolks, salt, milk, rum, lemon, bread crumbs, butter, sour cream;

Stuffing: 540 g ground walnut kernels, 150 g sugar, 80 g honey, 1 egg yolk, 2 eggs, milk, 2 tablespoons rum, 1 lemon, melted butter;

Knead the ingredients into a leavened dough as for the potica and leave it to rise in a warm place. If you bake it in a baker's oven, roll out the dough on an oven-peel, otherwise roll it out on a floured work surface and put it into a greased baking tin. Mix the ingredients for the stuffing into a smooth mixture and spread it on the dough. Fold the edges back over the stuffing. Leave it for a while until the edges are nicely risen. Bake it in the oven at 200°C for about 35 minutes. When it is finished, sprinkle it with icing sugar, cut it up and serve hot. If you have baked it in a baker's oven, serve it on the oven-peel (its name in Slovene originates from this method of serving).

Turnip Cake - Repinjača

Dough: 600 g wheat flour, 40 g fresh yeast, 100 g lard, 600 ml milk, salt, sugar;

Stuffing: 500 g raw turnips, 60 g lard, 2 tablespoons sugar, 4 eggs, 300 ml sour cream, grease;

Knead the ingredients to make a firm dough and leave it to rise. In the meantime, grate the turnips, salt them and leave them for at least 1 hour. After that, squeeze out the water and fry the turnip in lard until the water evaporates. Add the sugar and work in the eggs and the cream. Roll out the dough (a bit more than 1 cm thick) and put it in a greased baking tin or, for a baker's oven, a floured oven-peel. Spread the stuffing evenly over the dough. Mix the eggs into the cream and pour the mixture over the stuffing. Fold the edges over the stuffing and leave it to rise for a little longer. Bake it in the oven at 190°C for about 30 minutes. If you use a baker's oven, the cooking time is slightly shorter.

Povitice

1 kg husked millet, 250 g bacon, 250 g pork, 2 eggs, 600 g pork perotpneum, pimiento, marjoram, thyme, soup, salt, black pepper, garlic;

Wash the millet and half cook it in water, then leave it to cool. It is best if you use the water in which you cooked the cured pork meat. Mince the bacon and the pork and mix in the cold millet. Add the eggs, herbs, garlic and seasoning. If necessary, pour in some more soup, but be careful not to overdo it. The mixture should be thick. Wrap it in pork perotpneum and first cook it for approximately 15 minutes and then roast it in the oven at 180°C for about 1 hour. Serve cold with potato salad or warm with sauerkraut or sour turnip.

Tarragon Cake with Sour Cream

Dough: 200 g butter, 200 g flour, 200 g sugar, grated lemon peel, 2 eggs;

Stuffing: 50 g butter, 3 egg yolks, 250ml thick sour cream, 100 g sugar, whisked egg whites, 3 bunches chopped tarragon, 500 g cottage cheese;

1 packet dough (500 g)

Quickly knead all the ingredients to make short crust pastry. Shape it into a lump and leave it in the fridge for 1 hour. Roll it out about 1 cm thick and put it in a well greased round baking tin. Sprinkle the pastry with crumbled cottage cheese, cream in which you have whisked one egg, tarragon and sugar. Put a layer of ready-made dough as if making a gibanica, then another layer of stuffing and repeat until all the dough is used. Keep some cottage cheese aside and mix in the cream, egg yolks and tarragon and pour in the tin as the last layer. Cover with ready-made dough. Bake in the oven for 45 minutes at 180°C. Whisk an egg white and cover the cake, then leave it in the oven until nicely coloured. The cake is then finished. Serve hot or cold.

Koroška Walnut Rolls

Pastry: 500 g flour, 2 eggs, 30 g butter, water, salt;

Stuffing: 250 g ground walnuts, 1 egg, 125 ml milk, sugar, cinnamon, cloves, grated lemon peel, breadcrumbs;

Mix the pastry ingredients into a soft and smooth dough, then leave it to rest for 30 minutes. In the meantime, prepare the stuffing. Scald the walnuts with boiling milk and mix in the egg, sugar, cinnamon, cloves and grated lemon peel. Add the breadcrumbs only if the mixture is too watery. When the pastry is ready, thinly roll it out and put a tablespoon of stuffing every 3 or 4 cm on half of it. Cover with the other half, press firmly between the stuffing balls. Cut into squares. Cook them in salted boiling water for about 15 minutes then take them out and sprinkle them with breadcrumbs fried in butter.

Štruklji in Slovenia is made with various stuffings and served on its own or as a side dish. Usually it is made with thin unleavened dough, but also with leavened, corn, buckwheat and potato dough.

During the summer, sour milk is regularly on the menu on dairy farms. The sour cream which floats on the sour milk is skimmed off and used for dishes like cucumbers with cream, potatoes with green beans, or for cakes.

Štajerska Baked Štruklji

Pastry: 500 g flour, 2 eggs, 2 teaspoons oil, lemon juice, lukewarm water, salt;

Stuffing: 250 g cottage cheese, 1 egg, ground cinnamon, 125 ml fresh cream, 1 kg grated apples, 50 g raisins, 100 g sugar, breadcrumbs;

Knead all the necessary ingredients into a smooth pastry and leave it to rest for 30 minutes. In the meantime, prepare the stuffing. Mix together the cottage cheese, egg yolk, cinnamon and firmly whisked egg white. Thinly roll out the pastry, spread it with melted butter and the cottage cheese mixture, and sprinkle it evenly with the apples, raisins and sugar. Roll tightly and bake in the oven at 190°C for 45 minutes.

Cheese Pouring

500 g flour, 500 g cottage cheese, 750 ml milk, 120 g sugar, 4 eggs, 130 g butter, 100 ml sour cream, salt, oil, icing sugar to sprinkle;

Mix the egg yolks, sugar and butter into a creamy mixture. Firmly whisk the egg whites. Pour the milk into the cottage cheese and work in the flour, gradually folding in the egg mixture and egg whites. Pour the mixture into a well greased baking tin. Bake in a preheated oven at 200°C for 30 minutes. When the pouring is finished, spread on the sour cream, sprinkle with sugar and bake for 15 more minutes. Slice and serve warm.

Rečca

200 g ground walnuts or hazelnuts, 200 g raisins, 250 g breadcrumbs, 250 g butter, marjoram, 200 ml milk or wine, pork peritoneum;

Fry the breadcrumbs in butter and add marjoram while still hot. Cook the walnuts in boiling milk or wine for about 15 minutes until the mixture is thick. Soak the raisins in rum. Mix all the ingredients well and add sugar. Shape in a roll and wrap in pork peritoneum. Bake in the oven at 180°C for 30 minutes. When finished, slice and serve with tea, or as a side dish with venison.

Salted Buckwheat Cake

Dough: 700 g buckwheat flour, 800 g white flour, 5 tablespoons milk, 150 g butter, salt, 40 g fresh yeast;

Stuffing: 1 kg cottage cheese, 250 g sour cream, 3 eggs, salt;

Scald the buckwheat flour with boiling water and leave it to cool. Knead both kinds of flour, some butter, salt and yeast mixture into a smooth dough. Roll it out about 1/2 cm thick and cut it into several pieces the size of the baking tin. Put the first piece of dough in a well greased baking tin, pour melted butter over it and evenly spread the stuffing. Repeat until you run out of dough. The last layer should be the dough. Leave it to rest for 1 hour. Before putting it in the oven, cut it into pieces, pour over some more melted butter and thick sour cream. Bake in the oven at 190°C for about 1 hour.

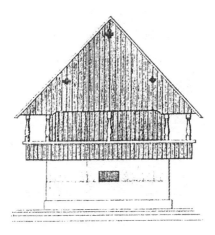

BREAD

The smell of freshly baked bread and the warmth of the farm stove make a home even cosier. Crops have not always been reliable in Slovenia so farmers have sown various types of cereals, resistant to the harsh weather conditions. To make enough bread for the whole family, they used different kinds of cereals, adding various other ingredients to make it even tastier.

Buckwheat Bread

500 g buckwheat flour, 1.5 kg white flour, 100 g yeast, 300 g ready-made mixture for mashed potatoes, 50 g salt, lukewarm water;

Sift all the flour, add the mashed potato mixture and mix well. Make a hole in the middle, add the oil, salt and yeast mixture. Form a dough, adding lukewarm water as necessary. Divide the dough into small loaves of about 300 g, cover them with a kitchen cloth and leave them in a warm place to rise. Once the dough has risen, place it on well greased baking tray and bake in the oven at 180°C for about 45 minutes. For corn bread, replace the buckwheat flour with corn flour scalded with boiling water.

Lizikina Cota

2 kg white bread, 500 ml milk, 4 eggs, ground cinnamon, 200 g sugar, salt;

Slice the bread and put the slices into an ovenproof dish. Whisk the eggs into the milk together with some salt and sugar and pour the mixture over the bread. Sprinkle with cinnamon and bake in the oven at 180°C for 45 minutes. Serve in slices with stewed fruit.

Lizikina cota is typical of the Velenje area and in Dobrovci near Miklavž na Dravskem polju.

Easter Bread

Dough: 500 g flour, 250 ml milk, 30 g fresh yeast, 80 g butter, 100 g sugar, salt, 2 eggs, grated lemon peel, 50 ml cherry brandy;

Stuffing: 200 ml wine, 150 g dry figs, 100 g dried apricots, 100 g hazelnuts, 20 g honey, cinnamon;

Make the dough in the same way as for the potica, only add cherry brandy. Finely chop the apricots, figs and hazelnuts, soak them in wine and add the honey and some cinnamon. Knead into a dough and shape into a loaf. Before putting it in the oven, make four lapels in the loaf with your thumb and index finger, then cut a cross between them. Spread with egg yolk and bake in the oven at 190°C for about 1 hour. In some parts of Primorska they used to bake this bread every Easter.

Zelan Bread

1 kg white flour, 50 g fresh yeast, 4 egg yolks, 300 ml lukewarm milk, 150 g butter, 80 g sugar, a handful of herbs (balm-mint, thyme, fennel), salt;

Knead the flour, yeast mixture, egg yolks and lukewarm milk into a dough, adding melted butter, sugar and lukewarm milk if necessary. Knead the dough until it is smooth, then cover it with a kitchen cloth and leave it in a warm place to rise for at least 1 hour. After that time knead the dough again, this time adding the herbs. Leave it again in a warm place to rise. Bake it as you would any other bread. When it is finished, cover it with a cloth, leave it to cool for a while and slice. This bread was always eaten up on the very same day it was made, when it was still slightly warm. This is also the origin of the saying – sunshine and neighbour's eyes hurt the Zelan bread. Zelan was in fact a special kind of herbal ceremonial bread, which used to be made every first Sunday after Easter.

White Bread

1 kg flour, 40 g fresh yeast, 40 g salt, 20 g sugar, about 400 ml lukewarm water;

Sift the flour into a bowl and make a hole in it in the middle. Crush the yeast, mix it with some flour and milk and pour the mixture in the hole. Dissolve the salt in warm water and pour the water in the hole. Knead to make a smooth non-sticky dough. Cover with a kitchen cloth and leave it in a warm place until it has doubled in size. If necessary, divide the dough into smaller loaves, knead them again and leave them to rise in a warm place. This time, leave it for a shorter period. If the bread has risen properly, it has a smooth crust, evenly spread holes and stays fresh longer. If the dough has been left to rise for too long, it will collapse and crack in the oven.

If you bake the bread in a baker's oven, put the loaves on a floured oven-peel and push them into the oven. If you bake it in an electric oven, put the dough into a baking tin and cut it 3 times with a knife.

Baking time varies depending on the size of the loaves. When the loaves are done, grease them to soften the crust, cover them with a table cloth and leave to cool.

Farm Bread

80 g butter, 200 ml milk, 100 g wheat germ, 350 ml beer, 40 g fresh yeast, 1 tablespoon honey, 30 g sugar, 700 g mixed wheat flour;

Heat the beer to 30 – 40°C and crumble in the fresh yeast. Leave it to rise, melt the butter in the milk, stir in the wheat germ and add the mixture to the beer. The milk mixture must not be too hot or it will destroy the yeast. Sift the flour,

Every farm has its own stove for baking bread. Freshly baked bread, just taken from the stove, smells wonderful …

add sugar and pour in the mixture. Knead into a dough. If it is too hard, add some water and if it is too sticky, add some flour. Knead well to get a smooth non-sticky dough. Leave it to rise for about 1 hour and knead it again. Divide into 2 loaves, leave them for about 1 more hour to rise and bake them in a preheated oven at 190°C for slightly less than 1 hour.

There are so many ways of making bread. Bread was traditionally baked at home, for daily use or on special occasions from various cereals and ingredients added to taste.

Poprtnik

1 kg wheat flour, 40 g fresh yeast, 20 g sugar, 100 g butter, 2 egg yolks, 300 ml milk, 1 egg to spread the dough with, salt;

Knead the ingredients into a leavened dough and leave it to rise. Take 3/4 of the dough, shape it into a loaf, put it into a greased baking tin and leave it to rise again. Take the remaining 1/4 of the dough and make bird shapes out of it. Stick the birds on the loaf, spread all together with a beaten egg and bake in a baker's or electric oven.

Apostolic Bread

750 g butter, 750 g flour, 3 tablespoons sugar, 1 tablespoon grated lemon peel, 1 tablespoon grated orange peel, 4 eggs, 2 tablespoons sour cream, salt, pinch of ground aniseed;

Whisk the butter until creamy, then stir in the sugar, grated lemon and orange peel, cream, salt and egg yolks. Fold in the firmly whisked egg whites and gently work in the flour to get a firm dough. Generously butter the baking tin and put in 2/3 of the dough and shape it into a loaf. Make a small dent into the loaf, cover it with melted butter and add the remaining dough, also shaped into a loaf. Butter again. Cover with a table cloth and leave in a warm place for 6 to 7 hours then bake it in the oven at 180°C for 1 hour. Serve at Easter with cured ham.

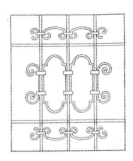

Walnut Bread

120 g flour, 4 eggs, 140 g chopped walnut kernels, 60 g breadcrumbs, 140 g sugar, salt, grated lemon peel;

Whisk the sugar and 4 egg yolks until creamy. Firmly whisk 4 egg whites and fold half of it into the whisked egg yolks. Add the walnuts, flour, breadcrumbs, lemon peel and the rest of the egg whites (fold the egg whites in very carefully or else the bread will be hard; the breadcrumbs to regulate the thickness of the dough). Put the dough in a well greased baking tin sprinkled with breadcrumbs and bake it at 180°C for 40 minutes.

Chocolate bread

70 g flour, 40 g chopped almonds or walnuts, 140 g sugar, 1 teaspoon vanilla sugar, 4 eggs, 150 g powdered chocolate;

Whisk the eggs, sugar and vanilla until you get a smooth creamy mixture. Gently fold in the chocolate, walnuts and flour. Put the mixture in a small greased baking tin sprinkled with breadcrumbs and bake in a preheated oven at 180°C for 40 minutes.

Corn Tepkanci

1 kg corn flour, 400 ml cream, 3 eggs, salt, black pepper, 1 teaspoon sugar, cabbage leaves;

Knead all ingredients into a firm dough. Leave it to rest in a cold place for half an hour. Make small balls from the dough, put them onto greased cabbage leaves in a well greased baking tin and leave them to rest for another half an hour. Bake them in the oven at 200°C for around 30 minutes. Cover them with cream a few times while they are baking to prevent cracks appearing in the dough. Sprinkle them with sugar and serve warm with white coffee or sprinkle them with black pepper and serve with sour milk or cottage cheese.

POTICE

with all kinds of stuffings are culinary masterpieces of Slovenia.

Walnut Potica

Dough: 1kg white flour, 50 g fresh yeast, 500 ml milk, 8 egg yolks, 2 packets vanilla sugar, grated lemon peel, 200 g sugar, 30 ml rum, 1 egg;

Stuffing: 1 kg ground walnut kernels, 250 g butter, 125 g cream, 8 egg whites, 100 ml rum, 1 lemon;

Sift the flour the evening before and leave it overnight in a warm place. Prepare the yeast mixture in the morning. Crush the yeast, pour in some milk, add the flour and sugar, mix well and leave it in a warm place to rise. In the meantime, mix 8 egg yolks, vanilla sugar, grated lemon peel, some rum, sugar and warm milk into the flour. Start kneading and after a while work in the yeast mixture. Knead for about 10 minutes until bubbles start appearing in the dough. Cover the dough with a kitchen cloth and leave it in a warm place for 1 hour, then knead it again and leave it to rise for another hour. While the dough is rising, prepare the stuffing. Boil the butter with the cream and pour the mixture onto the ground walnuts. Mix well and add the stiffly whisked egg whites, rum and lemon juice. Once again, mix well and leave it to cool slightly, so that the stuffing is tepid. When the dough doubles in size, roll it out (finger high), spread it with stuffing and tightly roll to make a potica. Grease a baking tray, sprinkle it with ground walnuts and put in the potica. Let it rise in a warm place for another 15 minutes. Before putting it in the oven, cover it with beaten egg or milk. In a baker's oven it takes about 1 – 1 1/2 hours. In an electric oven bake it for 1 hour, first at 200°C and then at 170°C. When it is finished, turn it out of the tray immediately and sprinkle with icing sugar. Cut it only when it is completely cold.

Pinca

1 kg white flour, 40 g fresh yeast, 3 eggs, 2 egg yolks, 100 g raisins, 100 g sugar, 10 g vanilla sugar, 80 g raisins, 100 ml milk, 50 ml brandy, salt, grated lemon peel;

Dilute the yeast and a tablespoon of sugar in lukewarm milk and leave the mixture in a warm place to rise. Sift the flour, add the yeast mixture, sugar, vanilla sugar, 2 eggs, egg yolks, melted butter, raisins, grated lemon peel, brandy and milk and knead to make a smooth dough. Knead again and shape into a loaf. Butter a baking tin, spoon the mixture in and leave it to rise for at least 20 minutes. Make three cuts in the centre of the loaf and spread it evenly with beaten egg. Bake it in the oven at 180°C for about 90 minutes.

Sprinkle the pinca with icing sugar while it is still hot.

Mlinčevka

Leavened dough: 350 g flour, 20 g fresh yeast, 100 ml milk, 2 egg yolks, 50 g butter, 40 g sugar, grated lemon peel;

Mlinci: 250 g flour, 1 egg, salt, lukewarm water, boiling milk;

Stuffing: 500 g cottage cheese, 100 g sugar, grated lemon peel, vanilla sugar, 250 g finely chopped walnut kernels, 300 ml sour cream, 100 g raisins or grapes, cinnamon;

Prepare the leavened dough in the same way as for potica. When it has risen, roll it out thinly and spread it in a baking tin. It has to cover the bottom, all the sides and hang for a few centimetres over the edges. Knead the dough for mlinci and leave it to rest for a while. Divide it into several portions and roll it out (about half a finger high) in the shape of the baking tin . Stretch the dough slightly with your hands and put it in a shallow baking tin, piercing it several times with a fork so it doesn't get bubbly while baking. Bake in the oven at 200°C until golden brown, leave to cool then scald with hot milk. To prepare the stuffing, mix together the cottage cheese, sugar, raisins, cinnamon, grated lemon peel, vanilla sugar and 200 ml of sour cream. Spread the stuffing on the leavened dough on the bottom of the baking tin, sprinkle with chopped walnuts and put on a mlinec. Spread it with the stuffing and sprinkle with walnuts again. Repeat until the tin is full, making sure that layers of stuffing are at least as thick as the mlinci between them. The higher the mlinčevka, the better. The top layer should be the stuffing which you cover with the leavened dough stretching over the edges. Pour over the rest of the sour cream and spread it evenly. Bake in the oven at 190°C for about 1 hour.

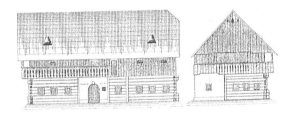

Potica with Dried Pears

Dough: 600 g white flour, 40 g fresh yeast, 3 egg yolks, 100 g butter, 50 ml rum, 200-300 ml lukewarm milk, grated lemon peel, salt, grease and breadcrumbs for the baking tin, egg white, icing sugar;

Stuffing: 500 g dried pears, 3 eggs, 100 g sugar, 50 ml rum, grated lemon peel, cinnamon;

Knead warm sifted flour, yeast mixture, salt, melted butter, egg yolks, sugar, rum, grated lemon peel and enough lukewarm milk to make a leavened dough. While the dough is rising, prepare the stuffing. The evening before making the potica wash the pears, remove the pips and soak them in water. Next morning cook them and leave them to cool. Finely chop the pears, put them in a bowl, add sugar, cinnamon, grated lemon peel, rum, egg yolks and stiffly whisked egg whites. Stir well to get a smooth mixture. Roll out the dough about 1 cm thick, spread it with the stuffing and roll tightly. Generously grease the baking tin and sprinkle it with bread crumbs. Carefully put in the potica and spread it with egg white, beaten egg or cream. Bake in a medium hot oven at 180°C for 1 hour. Take it out of the tin and sprinkle with icing sugar while still hot.

Tarragon Potica

Dough: 1 kg white flour, 40 g fresh yeast, 3 egg yolks, 300 ml lukewarm milk, 140 g butter, 1 teaspoon salt, 2 teaspoons sugar;

Stuffing: 150 g butter, 200 g sugar, 200 ml cream, 3 eggs, 2 handfuls chopped tarragon leaves;

Knead the ingredients into a soft leavened dough and leave it to rise. In the meantime, prepare the stuffing. Melt the butter and mix it with the egg yolks, cream and firmly whisked egg whites. Thinly roll out the dough, spread it with the stuffing and sprinkle with sugar and chopped tarragon leaves. Tightly roll it and put it in a greased baking tin. Leave it in a warm place to rise again. Before putting it in the oven, spread it with a beaten egg. Bake in a medium hot oven for about 1 hour. When it is finished, turn it out of the tin immediately and sprinkle it with icing sugar.

Metlika Špehovka

Dough: 500 g white flour, 30 g fresh yeast, 50 g sugar, 2 eggs, 50 g butter, 1 teaspoon rum, 300 ml milk, grated lemon peel, salt;

Stuffing: 300 g cracklings without lard, 4 eggs, 1 bunch of chives, 100 ml sour cream;

Melt the cracklings, stir in the eggs and chopped chives until you get a spreadable mixture. If the cracklings are too dry, add a tablespoon or two of sour cream.

Knead the rest of the ingredients into a leavened dough as for the potica. Make sure you use warm flour. Let the dough rise, knead it again and leave it to rise for a second time. Roll it out about 1 cm thick on a floured cloth. Spread on the stuffing and roll tightly. Put the špehovka in a greased baking tin, cover it with a kitchen cloth and leave it to rise for 30 minutes. Beat an egg and spread it on the špehovka before putting it in the oven. Bake it in the same way as a potica.

Honey Potica

Dough: 500 g flour, 250 butter, 15 tablespoons warm milk, 2 eggs, 40 g fresh yeast, salt, 2 tablespoons sugar;

Stuffing: 1 litre honey, 350 g ground walnuts, 3 tablespoons rum, 1 tablespoon ground cinnamon, 1 tablespoon grated lemon peel; crumbled biscuits

To make the dough, first work the butter into the flour, then add the yeast mixture, sugar, eggs and grated lemon peel. Make a smooth dough and leave it in a warm place to double in size. Knead it once more and leave it to rise again.

To prepare the stuffing, boil the honey and stir in the rest of the ingredients (except for the crumbled biscuits), but keep a few tablespoons of ground walnuts. Roll out the dough (about 1 cm thick), spread on the stuffing, sprinkle it with the remaining walnuts and crumbled biscuits and roll it tightly. Put the potica in a greased baking tin, leave it to rise for a while then coat it with a beaten egg and bake it in a preheated oven at 190°C for 1 hour.

Note: If you don't knead the dough enough, it will be coloured, humid and the holes in it will be unevenly spread. If you overdo the kneading, it will become floppy during rising because all the air has been squeezed out, resulting in a floppy final product. This usually happens if you prepare the dough in a food processor. If you knead the dough yourself, it is more likely to be underdone than overdone.

Koroška Šarkelj

Dough: 500 g flour, 3 egg yolks, 100 g butter, 30 g fresh yeast, 100 g sugar, 300 ml milk, salt;

Stuffing: 100 g sugar, 200 g raisins, ground cinnamon;

Cream the butter, mix in the egg yolks and sugar and finally the flour, yeast mixture, milk, salt, and knead into a smooth dough. Leave it to double in size then thickly roll it out and sprinkle it evenly with raisins, sugar and ground cinnamon. Roll it tightly, put into a round šarkelj baking tin and leave it to rise again. Coat it with beaten egg and bake in a preheated oven at 190°C for about 1 hour.

Layered Potica

Dough: 1 kg flour, 120 g butter, 4 egg yolks, 120 g sugar, 400 ml milk, 1 tablespoon rum, 40 g fresh yeast, 1 teaspoon salt;

Stuffing: 10 slices white bread (at least 1 day old), 4 eggs, 1 kg cottage cheese, 500 ml cooked cream, 100 g sugar, 50 g raisins, 150 g walnut kernels, lukewarm milk, grated lemon peel, ground cinnamon;

Make the yeast mixture and knead it with the flour and the rest of ingredients to make a leavened dough. Leave it to rise twice, kneading it in between. In the meantime, prepare the stuffing. Mix 1 egg with lukewarm milk and pour over the sliced bread. Put the cottage cheese in a separate bowl, add 3 beaten eggs and cooked cream, a few tablespoons of sugar, cinnamon, grated lemon peel and raisins soaked in rum. Roughly chop walnut kernels.

Knead the dough again and roll it out about 1 cm thick. Grease a baking tin and put in the dough so that about 1/3 of it is hanging over the edge of the tin. Sprinkle the dough in the tin with walnuts, cover with a layer of sliced bread and spread on about 1 cm thick layer of cottage cheese mixture. Repeat until you run out of the stuffing. Make sure that the potica is not higher than the baking tin. Cover with the dough, brush with beaten egg and leave it to rise for a while. Bake it in a preheated oven at 190°C for 45 minutes. Take it out, sprinkle with icing sugar, leave it to cool slightly, cut it and serve warm.

Štula – Potica with millet

Dough: 750 g white flour, 300 ml milk, 100 g lard or butter, 2 egg yolks, 40 g fresh yeast, 1 tablespoon sugar;

Stuffing: 1 kg pork head, 300 g husked millet, 2 eggs, 1 onion, 1 bunch parsley sprigs;

Prepare the leavened dough in the same way as that for špehovka.

To prepare the stuffing, first cook the pork. Take 500 ml of the remaining soup and cook the porridge oats in it. Add the finely chopped or minced pork, 2 eggs, finely chopped onion and parsley, marjoram and crushed garlic. Season with salt and pepper and mix well. Spread the stuffing on the rolled out dough, roll up and put in a well greased baking tin. Leave to rise for 30 minutes. Bake in the oven in the same way as špehovka. Just before it is done, pour the cream over.

PASTRY AND DESSERTS

Medvode Biscuits

250 g margarine for baking, 250 g vegetable lard, 1 egg, 1 packet baking powder, 400 g white flour, 1/2 packet vanilla sugar, 80 g sugar, 80 g jam, salt, icing sugar (optional)

Mix the vegetable lard, egg, vanilla sugar and sugar until the mixture is smooth and creamy. Salt to taste. Add flour and baking powder. Knead into a dough and roll it out on a floured surface about 3 to 5 mm thick. Take a brandy glass, cut out the biscuits and put them on a cold ungreased baking tray. Bake them in preheated oven at 190°C until golden brown. Take them out and leave them to cool, then coat half of them with diluted jam. Cover them with the other half of the biscuits and coat or sprinkle them with icing sugar if you wish.

Trieste Fave

300 g flour, 6 eggs, 120 g butter, 650 g peeled ground almonds, 1 kg icing sugar;

Mix all the ingredients together until firm and divide it into small balls. Put the balls on a greased baking tin and briefly bake them in the oven at 190°C. Sprinkle with icing sugar while they are still hot.

Martin's Apple

8 large apples, 500 g chestnuts, 50 g bacon;

Cut off the tops of the apples and hollow them. Fill the apples with cooked peeled chestnuts and cover with a slice of bacon. Put the apples in a greased baking tin and bake them in an electric or baker's oven.

Dressed Pears

Pastry: 300 g flour, 2 teaspoons baking powder, 2 packets vanilla sugar, 200 g butter, 250 g cottage cheese, pinch of salt;

Stuffing and pears: 100 g almonds, 170 g sugar, 125 ml fresh cream, 4 large pears, 250 ml white wine, 2 eggs, grated lemon peel, 2 tablespoons milk, ginger;

Mix the ingredients necessary for pastry. For the best results, prepare it the day before. You could also use ready- made pastry from a shop in which case you would need you need 1 (500 g) packet. Peel the pears, halve them and remove the pips. Put the water, wine, 50 g of sugar and grated lemon peel into a saucepan and bring to the boil, then add the pears and cook for 8 to 10 minutes. Take them out and leave them to cool. In the meantime, prepare the caramel almonds. Put the rest of the sugar in a pan and melt it on a low flame until liquid. Stir in the almonds and fry them stirring constantly until golden brown. Whip the cream, carefully fold it in and simmer until you get a thick stuffing for the

Doughnuts, flancati and various biscuits were usually made on Shrove Tuesday, but they were always served at other festive occasions as well.

pears. Cut the pastry into 4 big squares in which you will wrap the pears. Spread the edges with egg white. Fill the pear halves with the almond stuffing and stick them together again. Wrap them in pastry, firmly press the edges together, then coat with a mixture of egg and milk. Bake the pears in the oven at 200°C for about 30 minutes. Take them out and sprinkle with icing sugar. This dish goes nicely with vanilla sauce.

Stuffed Apples

4 large apples, grated lemon peel, 4 cloves, 150 g sugar, 3 eggs, 50 g raspberry or any other jam, 100 g peeled almonds, 30 g breadcrumbs, whipped cream;

Peel the apples and remove the centre with the pips. Cook them in water with some sugar, grated lemon peel and cloves. When the apples are cooked, take them out and put them in a deep baking tin. Half fill them with jam. To prepare the stuffing, mix 100 g sugar, 3 egg yolks, 1 egg white and almonds. Firmly whisk the remaining two egg whites and gently fold them into the almond mixture together with breadcrumbs. Fill the apples with the stuffing, putting some of it on top of them as well. Bake them in the oven. Take them out and cover with whipped cream in which you have mixed a tablespoon of sugar.

Creamy Biscuits

550 g flour, 1/2 packet baking powder, 200 ml sour cream, 100 g butter, 1 tablespoon rum, 1 egg, 2 egg yolks;

Mix the flour with the baking powder, make a hole in the centre and add the cream, eggs, rum, sugar and diced butter. Knead to make a smooth dough, divide it in two and leave it to rest for half an hour. Roll it out, cut out the biscuits, put them on a greased baking tray and bake them in the oven until they become light yellow.

Brown Honey Biscuits

250 g honey, 100 g sugar, 200 g fried almonds, juice of 1 lemon, 300 g flour, 1/2 packet baking powder, ground cinnamon;

Bring the honey to the boil, add the sugar, almonds, lemon juice, cinnamon, flour and baking powder. Knead to make a firm dough and leave it to rest for a few hours. Roll it out about 5 mm thick and cut it into small rectangles. Bake them on a greased floured tray in the oven at 190°C for 15 minutes. Before taking them out, coat them with honey diluted with 1 tablespoon of water.

Yoghurt Mice

1 yoghurt, 1 egg, 1 packet baking powder, 1 packet vanilla sugar, 1 teaspoon rum, 2 tablespoons sugar, 10 tablespoons flour, pinch of salt, icing sugar to sprinkle;

Mix all the ingredients together in a blender to get a smooth dough. Heat the oil. To test the heat of the oil, put in a teaspoon of dough into the pan. If the dough gets a nice, even, golden colour the oil has the right temperature. Take a large tablespoon, dip it in the hot oil and put one tablespoon of dough at a time into the oil and fry until golden brown. Take them out and put on a strainer so the oil drips away. Sprinkle with icing sugar while still hot.

If preparing a large quantity of dough, use half of the amount of rum and baking powder than indicated in the recipe.

Pastry Flancati

1 kg flour, 600 ml thick sour cream, 8 egg yolks, 100 g sugar, 2 tablespoons lemon juice, 2 tablespoons rum, 6 tablespoons wine, frying oil, icing sugar;

Quickly knead the ingredients to make a smooth pastry and leave it to rest. Roll it out very thinly and cut it into rectangles with a pastry cutting wheel. Make 3 or 4 cuts in each rectangle. Interweave the strips and deep fry the flancati. Take them out and put them on a strainer so that the excess oil drips away. Sprinkle them with sugar while they are still warm.

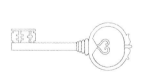

Dolenjska Flancati

500 g flour, 100 g butter, 150 g sugar, 2 eggs, 150 ml cream, 2 tablespoons rum, 100 ml white wine, 1 teaspoon baking powder, salt, icing sugar, frying oil;

Whisk the butter, sugar, eggs and salt into a creamy mixture and add the cream, rum and wine. Carefully work in the flour, mixed with baking powder. The dough must be soft and smooth. Cover it and leave to rest for 1 hour in a warm place. Thinly roll out the dough on a floured surface. Cut it into 3 x 6 cm pieces and make 2 to 3 incisions into each of them. Put the edges through the holes and fry them in oil, shaking the pan so that the flancati expand nicely. Sprinkle them with vanilla flavoured icing sugar while they are still hot.

Shrove Tuesday Doughnuts

1 kg flour, 60 g fresh yeast, 250 ml milk, 250 ml cream, 1 egg, 100 g sugar, orange or lemon peel, nutmeg, salt, 4 tablespoons rum, 150 g butter, apricot jam, frying oil, icing sugar;

Sift the flour and prepare the yeast mixture. Whisk the egg yolks, the egg and sugar to a creamy mixture. Grate the lemon or orange peel and the nutmeg. Warm up the milk and the cream. Mix all that into a leavened dough, then add the melted butter. The dough should be soft or else the doughnuts will be heavy. Don't knead the dough but beat it with a wooden spoon. Don't raise it too high to prevent air bubbles in the dough and consequently in the doughnuts. When the dough stops sticking to the bowl and the wooden spoon, cover it with a table cloth and leave it in a warm place to rise. Put the risen dough on a floured wooden tray or kitchen cloth. Roll it out about 5 mm thick and cut out the doughnuts. Put a teaspoon of jam on half of them and cover with the remaining half so that the upper part of the dough covers the jam. Press firmly together around the edges and then cut the edges off with a slightly smaller doughnut cutter. The edges have to be pressed together really firmly to prevent jam leaks, and the jam has to be in the centre otherwise the doughnuts will turn around in the oil. Put the prepared doughnuts on a floured tablecloth, cover them and leave them to rise.

Take a pan and pour in the oil about 5 cm high. First try frying only one doughnut, putting it in oil with the upper, more risen side, down. Cover with a lid and fry. When it is nicely coloured, turn it around and fry it again. If they have risen properly, they will only half sink in the oil and when you turn them around they get a nice white stripe all around. If they have risen too much, they will sink, there will be no white stripes and they will turn in the oil. If the oil is too hot, the dough gets coloured much faster than it is actually cooked. To see if the dough is fried, take a knitting needle and stick it into a doughnut from the side. If there is dough on it when you take it out, the doughnut is not done. Make sure the doughnuts don't touch in the pan. When you take them out, put them on a strainer until the excess oil drips away and sprinkle them with sugar while they are still warm.

HERBS AND SPICES USED IN SLOVENIAN CUISINE

Dill (Anethum graveolens)
In the kitchen, seeds, dried leaves and freshly chopped leaves are used. Aneth seeds are well known for their positive effects on appetite and digestion.

Angelica (Angelica archangelica)
Cook the stems and roll them in crystal sugar in order to preserve them for longer. They can be used as decoration for desserts. Fresh leaves are added to sour dishes for a milder taste and in order to reduce the amount of added sugar needed. It is also used in jams and different drinks, especially in summer. Cooked stems and roots can also be used as a vegetable.

Chervil (Anthriscum cerfolium)
It is a perennial plant and one of the first to come out in spring. It is used in the same way as parsley and chopped on salads.

Tarragon (Arthemisia drancunculus)
Its sophisticated smell makes it one of the essential herbs in the kitchen. It is used to scent vinegar, added to different sauces and in other dishes.

Borage (Borago officinalis)
It is up to 50 cm high with velvety grey-green leaves and wonderful star-like purple blossoms. Its leaves are used with smothered meat or can be stuffed (in the same way as vine leaves). It is also used for soups and its taste resembles that of cucumber.

Tansy (Chryzanthemum vulgare asperula odorata)
It has a very rich yellow blossom, made of a number of smaller button-like blossoms. It is a herb of bitter taste. Young leaves and shoots are used in salads, omelettes and various desserts, as well as for stuffing pasta.

Coriander (Coriandrum sativum)
It originates in the Middle East and Southern Europe. It is a very attractive plant with white, pink or pale yellow blossoms and delicate light green leaves which resemble that of parsley. All parts of the plant can be used in cooking. The leaves have a light flavour of anise, the seeds are sweet and resemble orange peel. Chopped roots have a strong smell and taste.

Fennel (Foenculum vulgare / F.v. dulce)
The whole plant is used: blossoms, stem, tiny leaves and bulbous bottom parts. It has a slightly sweet taste and smells like anise. It is used in seafood dishes, sauces, meat, sauerkraut, cabbage, or on its own.

Hyssop (Hyssopus officinalis)
It is an ornamental plant with an attractive smell, often used in Arabic cooking. In the kitchen, we use theleaves in soups, meat dishes, cheeses, sauces and pasta.

Bay Leaf (Laurus nobilis)
It is a bushy tree with smooth dark green leaves. In the kitchen its leaves are indispensable; we add them to soups, meat, sauces and fish dishes.

Lovage (Levisticum officinale)
It is a perennial plant resembling celery. In the kitchen we use its leaves, roots and seeds, but since its flavour disappears if cooked for too long, we always add it when the dish is nearly cooked. It is used in soups, salads, meat dishes and sauces.

Balm-mint (Melissa officinalis)

It is a plant with pleasant smelling blossoms and aromatic leaves. It is used with egg omelettes, tea and milky drinks, soups, vegetable dishes and venison.

Peppermint (Mentha)

There are various sorts of peppermint. In the kitchen, we mostly use dried or fresh leaves. It is added to fowl, fish, preserved fruit, desserts based on lemon and different cakes.

Basil (Ocimum basilicum)

In Greek, its name means "king" which is proof enough of its appreciation among people. In the kitchem we mostly use fresh or dried leaves, which we add to tomato sauces, fish, mushroom dishes, soups, meat sauces, salads, fowl, rice dishes, and it also goes well with other herbs and spices.

Marjoram and Oregano (Origanum majarana/ O. vulgare / O. onites)

These two perennial plants are closely related. We use fresh or dried leaves and add them to various salad dressings, fish dishes, soups, venison, mushroom sauces and tomato sauces.

Parsley (Petroselinum crispum)

Parsley is very widely used in Slovenia. The whole plant can be used, leaves and root, in vegetable dishes. It is also added to sauces and meat and fish dishes.

Rosemary (Rozmarinus officinalis)

It is a plant with a very strong flavour which is very important in fish, meat and fowl dishes as well as sauces, vegetables and potato dishes. It can also be added to some teas.

Sage (Salvia officinalis)

It is a medium sized bushy perrenial plant whose leaves have a very strong flavour. It is one of the most used herbs all over the world. Fresh or dried leaves make a welcome addition to various stuffings, pork meat, rice dishes, mushroom dishes, salads and cucumbers.

Calamint (Satureia hortensis)

It is one of the typical Mediterranean plants. Dried leaves keep their smell for a very long time. It is added to leguminous plants, vegetable salads, meat, sauces, cheeses and fish.

Thyme (Thymus vulgaris)

There are around a hundred sorts of thyme known to man. Strongly flavoured green leaves are of oval shape and up to 1 cm long. It can be added to almost any dish, but it is mostly used with dishes that have to be cooked slowly, sauces, various vegetable dishes, fish and fowl specialities.

Mustard (Brassica nigra)

This plant grows up to 2 m high. We only use its seeds, either made into mustard, or freshly ground and added to meat dishes, sauces and smoked fish. Mustard shoots make an excellent addition to fresh salads.

Cumin (Carum carvi)

It is a biennial plant which can grow up to 60 cm high and has small carved leaves and white or brownish blossoms. In the kitchen we mostly use the seeds, ground or whole, but also the chopped leaves, which we add to salads, and roots which can be cooked and used as a vegetable.

Cinnamon (Cinnamomum zeylanicum)

This sweet scent of the cinnamon tree bark originates in Sri Lanka. Ground cinnamon is added to meat, vegetable and sweet dishes. It is also excellent in fruit juices and with sweet potatoes.

Saffron (Crocus sativus)

These are crocus pistils with furrows which have a characteristically yellow colour and sharp taste. They have to be hand-picked. It takes one quarter of a million of crocus blossoms to make 250 g of saffron powder. In the kitchen we use the blossoms or the powder, adding it to soups, paella, meat dishes and sweet breads.

Juniper berries (Juniperus communis)

Juniper berries are the fruits of small evergreen bushes, which turn dark purple when ripe. While fresh berries cannot be used because their taste is too strong, dried berries have a nice flavour, slightly resembling stone pines. To bring out their flavour we have to crush them before use. We add them to marinades (venison), cabbage, meat dishes. They are also used for distilling brandy.

In winter time, workers who came from the forest were served black pudding and sauerkraut, home made black bread and zaseka.

Poppy Seeds (Papaverum sommiferum)
The seeds of the opium poppy whose Latin name suggests its narcotic powers are what we mainly use as a spice. European varieties usually have grey-blue seeds, while yellow and brown seeds can be found with other sorts as well. The seeds can be used whole or ground. Poppy seed oil is used in mild salad dressings. Poppy seeds are used to improve the taste of breads, desserts, sauces, pasta and vegetables.

Pimiento (Pimenta officinalis / P. diolca)
We can use whole or ground berries as a spice. They are added to spice mixtures for fruit or vegetable preservation, marinades for fish or shellfish, meat, venison, vegetables, rice, pies, soufflés and biscuits.

Anise (Pimpiela anisum)
Anise is botanically related to fennel, cumin and caraway seed. The plant grows up to 60 cm in height, its leaves resemble that of the coriander and it has flat yellow white blossoms. It originates in the Middle East. In some countries it is a popular addition to alcoholic beverages. If you scald the anise seeds with hot water, take out the seeds, sweeten the remaining liquid with honey and drink it, it will stimulate your digestion. In the kitchen we use dried seeds and fresh leaves. It is added to desserts, fish and shellfish, escargots, tomato sauces and vegetable dishes.

Black Pepper (Piper nigrum)
Pepper shrubs originate in equatorial forests of India. In the kitchen we use fresh green pepper corns, mixed corns, dried green corns, pink pepper corns, and green pepper corns in saltwater. The corns can be used whole or ground in all kinds of dishes.

Sesame oil (Sesamum indicum)
It originates in China. Sesame is up to 1 m high annual plant with egg-like thick leaves and white and pink blossoms. The seeds are harvested when the ripe seed bulbs break open. They can then be used for the production of sesame oil which tastes of walnuts and is used for sweet and spicy dishes. The seeds can be used whole or ground and we add them to desserts, breads, vegetables, green beans, meat, rice, noodles and some meat dishes.

Garlic (Allium sativum)
It originates in Eastern India. The whole plant can be used. The upper part of it can be used before blossoming as asparagus or in salad. The cloves contain ethe-real oil. Garlic is used in salads, sauces, side dishes and meaty dishes.

Chives (Allium tuberosum)
It originates in China and Japan. Its leaves resemble grass, and the bulb is up to 2 cm wide. There are several sorts of chives. Fresh leaves are added to salads, soups, side dishes or in other dishes.

Onion (Allium cepa)

It is thought to originate in Asia. Its leaves are round and hollow and can be eaten while young. There are many sorts of onions. It is used with meat dishes, salads, side dishes; it can be used raw, cooked, scalded or fried.

Leek (Allium porrum)

It is not known as a wild plant and could have come from a sort of onion. Its bulb grows into a thick stem, composed of long leaves, squeezed together. We use the whole plant for soups, side dishes, and as a delicacy, roasted in the oven, cooked with butter or sauces, or fried.

Cucumber (Cucumis sativus)

It originates in Eastern India. There are many varieties of the species. We use the pulpy oblong fruit, either raw in salads, cooked as a side dish, fried, roasted or smothered.

Pumpkins (Cucurbitaceae)

We know many varieties of pumpkins, some of which can weigh up to 100 kg. Others are marrows, zucchinis, white flat "White Bush" pumpkins, West Indian pumpkins, butternut pumpkins, etc. We use their pulp and they can keep for months in a dark cold cellar. Their pulp can be used cooked and with sugar as compote, cooked as a side dish or even pickled. It can also be steamed, roasted, grilled or used for soufflés or jams, as well as raw in salads. There are few other vegetables which can be prepared in as many different ways as this one.

Broad beans (Vicia faba)

It originates in the Middle East and is a climbing plant reaching up to 1m high. We can use green, not yet ripe, beans as a side dish, while ripe beans are traditionally mashed and served with ham and bacon. They are sold frozen or preserved, and fresh in the Summer. The shells are usually discarded, but if they are very young, we can use them. The most common variety is the Egyptian brown variety called 'gul'.

Peas (Pisum sativum)

We use young pods or freshly shelled beans in the same way as beans, broad beans, or dried peas, which can be blue, green, yellow, etc.

Lentils (Lens ensulenta)

Lentils originate in Asia which explains why a number of varieties are called dal. Lentils are especially rich in protein. There are large and small varieties. They all have the same flat round shape but they are of different sizes and colours: yellow, green, brown, dark brown, orange and yellow. They are served mashed in curry, and some varieties keep their shape during cooking. Lentils are the only leguminous plant which do not require soaking before cooking. The best known varieties are puy lentils, Indian brown lentils, sweet corn (Zea mays). Corn in Slovenia was also called turščica or debelača. It originates in Mexico, but today there are numerous varieties grown all over the world. It is available in grains or pods, either raw, frozen, or in cans. It is one of the most important sources of grains, corn meal and flour. It can be used in soups, side dishes and mashed, roasted or cooked. Various dishes can be made from its flour – polenta, porridge, corn syrup and bread.

Buckwheat (Fagopyrum ecsulentum)

Its grains are fried and ground into flour, which is then used for pancakes, crispy thin cakes, potice, žgance, and, in Japan, for soba noodles. It can also be used in soups and porridges.

Barley (Hordeum vulgare)

Barley flour can be used for baking bread, while barley porridge is used in stews.

Pot barley

Pot barley is finely crushed and polished barley, used in soups, stews or as pilav instead of rice.

Wheat

Wheat was probably originally cultivated along the Nile. It is ground into flour, which is used for making bread and pasta. The macoh flour, used for making unleavened crispy bread, is one of the best known varieties in the world. Burgul is cooked, dried, peeled and crushed wheat which is very popular in the Eastern Mediterranean and Middle East. They put it in pilav, soak and prepare as salad or make pasta out of it and serve it with lamb (Lebanese kibbi).

Oats (Avena sativa)

Oats originate in Europe. They are ground to a more or less fine flour. If we cook it in water it becomes soggy. It is made into porridge oats, added to bread dough and used in different cakes.

Bran

Bran is the outer layer of every cereal, which is usually removed from the grain when it is being ground into flour. It is a very valuable source of ballast and can be used ground into bran flour.

Millet (Panicum milliaceum)

It originates in Asia. It is just as rich in protein as wheat but because it lacks gluten it is not suitable for baking. Millet flour can be use for making mlinci or ponvičniki. It can be mixed with leguminous plants and vegetables, used for stews and milk porridge together with wheat.

Sorghum (Sorghum vulgare)

It is a variety of millet, cultivated in Africa and Asia. Ground grains are used for bread, porridge and flat biscuits as well as soups. Some varieties are used to make sweet syrup.

Rye (Secale cereale)

It probably originates in South-Western Asia and consists of similar ingredients to wheat. It is ground into flour which is used for baking rye bread. It is also used in the distillation of spirits.

Paprika (Capsicum annum)

It originates in tropical America and Western India. There are several varieties which differ in shape, colour, taste, size and flavour. It is available all year round. Sweet paprika has a mild taste and is used in various dishes while chilli peppers are hot and almost exclusively used only as a spice. It can be used raw or dried and ground.

Tomato (Lycopersicum esculentum)

It originates in South America. Botanically it is a berry and related to the potato. There is a great choice of varieties which differ in shape, size, succulence, colour and pulp. It is available all year round, raw or canned. Red tomatoes are used for salads, juice, puree or ketchup. Green tomatoes are usually pickled or used in chutneys.

Egg plant (Solanum Melongena)

It originates in India and comes in different shapes and colours. Its floury yellow-green pulp can be enjoyed cooked, fried, in combination with other vegetables or stuffed. It is typically used for moussaka, ratatouille and imam bajildi.

KAZALO POGLAVIJ

Glossary:

Zaseka: Recipe is on page 17
Mlinci: Mlinci are made of leavened dough (similar to dough for bread), baked in the oven, broken into small pieces and scalded with boiling salted water before serving. They are usually improved with gravy or 'zaseka'.

Soup vegetables: vegetables usually used in making soups. Depending on the season this can be carrots, parsley root, onion, bay leaf, garlic clove, thick turnip slice, celery, kale leaf.

Questions about Slovenia

It provides answers to numerous questions about Slovenia
and Slovenes living in their native and neighbouring countries
as well as abroad.

The booklet is about holidays, wine, the sea, mountains,
forests, rivers, early and recent history, cuisine, tourism, the
legal system, politics, humour, envy, cleverness, sadness,
drinking problems, superstition...

(112 pages, 150 colour photographs, a map, format 11.5
x 22.5 cm, paperback)

Slovenian Cooking

The booklet details 140 old and not so old national
dishes, which cherish a rich tradition in Slovenia.
Throughout the centuries some of them have managed to
preserve themselves to this day. A different ground structure
and varying climate in some areas as well as economic and
cultural factors have contributed their part in creating 40
culinary regions. These are characterized by different eating
habits and typical dishes.

140 recipes of both very well and less known Slovene
dishes have been collected by a chef, Andrej A. Fritz, 2001

(64 pages, format 11.5 x 22.5 cm, paperback)

Slovenia - Guide

The booklet is a brief presentation of Slovenia and its
principal characteristics. The texts are complemented by
150 colour photographs and a small but clear map of
Slovenia.

The introductory part is general, and includes basic
information about Slovenia, its tourism, history, arts and
crafts, cuisine... The following chapters present individual
regions, bigger towns and other sights of interest.

(112 pages, 150 colour photographs, a map, format
11.5 x 22.5 cm, paperback)

A road map of Slovenia and Istria

Maps of the following city centres: Ljubljana, Maribor,
Celje, Kranj and Koper
(scale:1:300,000, format 100 x 70)

Trstenik 101 SI-4204 Golnik
e-mail: info@zalozba-turistika.si
www.zalozba-turistika.si